BPMN
Modeling
and Reference Guide

BPMN Modeling

and Reference Guide

UNDERSTANDING AND USING BPMN

Develop rigorous yet understandable graphical
representations of business processes

STEPHEN A. WHITE, PHD
DEREK MIERS

Future Strategies Inc.
Lighthouse Point, Florida, USA

BPMN Modeling and Reference Guide:
Understanding and Using BPMN

Copyright © 2008 by Future Strategies Inc.

ISBN10: 0-9777527-2-0
ISBN13: 978-0-9777527-2-0

Published by Future Strategies Inc., Book Division

2436 North Federal Highway, #374,
Lighthouse Point, FL 33064 USA
954.782.3376 / 954.782.6365 fax
www.FutStrat.com — books@FutStrat.com
Cover: Hara Allison www.smallagencybigideas.com

Publisher's Cataloging-in-Publication Data

ISBN: 978-0-9777527-2-0
Library of Congress Control Number: 2008932799

**BPMN Modeling and Reference Guide: Understanding and Using BPMN
/Stephen A. White, PhD., Derek Miers
p. cm.**

Includes bibliographical references and appendices.
1. Business Process Management. 2. Process Modeling. 3. Enterprise Architecture. 4. Notation Standard. 5. Workflow. 6. Process Analysis

White, Stephen A.; Miers, Derek

BPMN Modeling and Reference Guide
Table of Contents

Foreword

Richard Mark Soley, Ph.D.

Chairman and CEO
Object Management Group, Inc.
July 2008

Cheaper by the dozen! What kind of crazy couple would carefully plan out their family to include a dozen children, simply because their detailed study of child-rearing had computed a family of twelve children to be optimal? Only a man and woman so deeply steeped in time-and-motion studies that their entire life revolved around optimization. Though the family of Frank and Lillian Gilbreth has been celebrated on the silver screen, the dehumanizing effects of the view of people as cogs in the machine has also found its way to the klieg lights, most obviously in Charlie Chaplin's dark comedy "Modern Times."

Clearly the optimization of business processes is not a particularly new idea. The Industrial Revolution, especially in the late 19th century, focused attention on the systemization of business to increase revenue and profits, resulting in not only Colt's and Ford's standardized parts and assembly lines, but also the time-and-motion studies of the Gilbreths and Frederick Winslow Taylor. Under the headings of "ergonomics" and "human-factors design," these studies continue to optimize shipping departments, manufacturing organizations, healthcare provision, even automotive design.

What about optimizing management practice? Certainly the revolution leading to the common Western management style of the early 20th century put in place a structure that seems quite rigid from the outside, though that rigidity is rarely visible inside. Management is often regarded often as a "soft" science, though certainly decision-making efficacy and efficiency can be measured (and are, in some firms).

At the core of business process optimization has to be a focus on systemizing business practice, whether that practice is the daily function of a telemarketer in a call center, a shipping clerk on the loading dock, an appointments manager in a medical office, or a Vice President finalizing an investment decision. Even decision-making processes that cannot be fully automated can nonetheless be mapped, tracked, optimized and edited. The science for doing so is not particularly new; the systems to support managing business processes are not even new. What's new is a focused interest in leveraging a specific management practice to support business agility—and a worldwide standard for specifying business processes, whether they be fully automated, completely manual, or somewhere in-between.

The Business Process Modeling Notation (BPMN) is the culmination of two streams of work from the late 1990's and early in this century. One of those streams was focused on workflow management and planning, while the other was concerned with modeling and architecture. It is amazing to note that after hundreds of years of success in the careful design engineering of bridges, ships and buildings from the 16th century forward, so-called "modern" engineering disciplines like software development have successfully resisted ancient and relevant engineering discipline for decades. This is changing—the recognition that modeling is necessary to the success of large complex software systems is now quite common, just as it became a common recognition in the shipwrights and building trades in the 16th and 17th centuries, and the bridge-builder's trade in the 19th century. Blueprints are just as relevant to software as they are to building designs.

From an abstract viewpoint, software designed to run businesses (like enterprise resource planning systems, shipment management systems, billing systems and the like) are in fact business process descriptions at a startlingly low level. You wouldn't know by looking at the arcane C++ and Java codes that these systems described business processes, but of course they do. In fact, even BPMN business process descriptions are a generalization of what software is about—automating processes. But real processes in real organizations aren't fully automatable. Which means we can't use the same language to define, can't use the same processes to measure, or to optimize. The combination of the ability of "modern" program languages to obscure the intention of function, with their inability to clearly integrate manual and executive processes, makes most programming languages at least inefficient and more likely useless as process description languages.

This technical stream of practice description, along with the late 20th century trends of workflow management and Business Process Re-engineering, forged the appearance of an explicit and detailed language to describe business processes, focusing on clearly stating the intent of a process description and fully recognizing that all interesting business processes involve a human touch.

The merger of the Business Process Management Initiative (BPMI) with the Object Management Group (OMG) brought together two well-focused groups into a stronger organization. BPMI had focused on business processes; OMG had focused on the generic

BPMN Modeling and Reference Guide

modeling problem with its Model Driven Architecture, and especially on the modeling of software systems. The new OMG which emerged in 2005 successfully created a single organization focused on the modeling of systems, including business processes, in two dozen vertical markets from healthcare to finance, manufacturing to life sciences, and government systems to military systems. Not only did the BPMN language stay, but it gained a detailed technical underpinning with MDA (integrating it with languages for expressing software design, systems engineering design and even hardware design). Most importantly, the expertise stayed with the language--invaluable expertise in business modeling, scarce in OMG before the merger, is now central to OMG's success.

This book represents in clear and certain terms the expertise of two of those experts, with a reference not only of the where's and why's of BPMN but more importantly the how's. How do I represent various sorts of processes? How do I know when I've done it right? How do I get value from those process descriptions, and measure and optimize the resulting processes? No-one knows better how to answer these questions than Stephen White and Derek Miers, so if an optimized business is what you're looking for, you've got the right book in yours hands.

Angel Luis Diaz, Ph.D.

Director, Websphere Business Process Management
IBM Software Group
August 2008

The business landscape is full of challenges, uncertainties and opportunities. For many companies and industries, these changes are becoming more significant—even transformative—in nature. Business Process Management (BPM) helps an organization's business processes become more flexible and responsive to change. BPM is a discipline, combining software capabilities and business expertise to accelerate process improvement and facilitate business innovation.

Standards for BPM help the organization harness the power of change through their business processes, leveraging a Service Oriented Architecture (SOA) to quickly accommodate changing business conditions and opportunities.

In a rapidly evolving business climate, the proactive development and use of standards are key to remaining competitive for both BPM vendors and their customers. Process-oriented standards enable organizations to connect the business functions together, both internally and externally with their customers, partners, and suppliers. It's not about technology for the sake of technology—it's about enabling new ways of doing business. It's about helping an organization to reach new levels of innovation while continuing to deliver the increases in productivity that are necessary to improve the bottom line. Open standards enable business to lower costs, increase revenue and respond quickly to industry pressures.

What is new is that the open standards are now getting closer to business intent, and the pace at which they are emerging is accelerating driven by the layering that occurs. As one set of best practices is agreed, it opens the door to the next opportunity for innovation while leveraging the increasing base of open integration, connectivity, and interoperability standards. With the wide spread adoption of Service Oriented Architecture standards (e.g. XML, Web Services...) we now have a solid foundation to build standards for Business Process Management.

This leads us to the Business Process Modeling Notation (BPMN), one of the key standards that has emerged in the BPM space. BPMN improves organizational BPM efforts by providing a common graphical language, facilitating communication and a better understanding of business processes in both business and IT.

The future of BPMN is bright as we further extend the "rigor" associated with business definition. This rigor will ensure that the investments business people make in defining their processes are quickly translated into reality. Moreover, through points of agility embedded right into the executing process, systems are easily optimized.

Business Process Management puts the business requirements in the driver seat; ensuring clarity of thought across all stakeholders from business leaders, analysts and users, all the way to information technology leaders and developers. I am personally very excited over the publication of this book as it will most definitely help bring BPM power to the masses and provide a valuable resource for all who are developing BPMN models and implementations.

Part I.   Understanding BPMN

Chapter 1.   Introduction

This book provides a modeling guide and reference for the features of BPMN Version 1.1.

In Part I, we describe a little of business drivers associated for process modeling, aligning that with the history of the Business Process Modeling Notation (BPMN™),[1] standard and discussing expected future developments. We go on to talk about processes and modeling in general to set up and position some of the issues and challenges for BPMN modelers.

We then present the BPMN modeling approach using a progressive scenario that unfolds for the reader. As we elaborate on each new aspect of the scenario, we feature the functionality of BPMN that supports the desired behavior. Rather than attempting to explain fully each concept in detail, this part of the book sticks to the fundamental principles, referring the reader to the relevant Reference Section for more detail (i.e., Part II of this book).

The intention is to enable the reader to understand how to apply BPMN against a real world scenario. Moreover, the approach taken here introduces each set of functionality in a non threatening way, allowing the reader to develop their understanding at their own pace. Throughout this part of the book, we introduce exercises for the reader to complete, helping them cement their comprehension and establish a fundamental level of skill. The answers to those exercises will be made available online (as part of the online training that complements this book).

Part II presents a detailed reference section that covers the precise semantics of the BPMN standard, explaining them and the process behavior that results.[2]

For the casual modeler, Part I will provide enough to get up and going. Over time, we expect that you will dip into Part II (the detailed reference) section to familiarize yourself with the precise functionality of the Notation.

---

[1] BPMN™ is a Registered Trademark of the Object Management Group.

[2] The BPMN specification itself and a list of vendors who support it are available at http://www.bpmn.org/. We chose not to include a list of vendors in this book as it would quickly become out of date.

Book Structure

The book is organized into 13 main chapters followed by Appendices, a Prologue, Glossary and Index:

Part I Chapter 1—"Introduction"

Chapter 2—"Process Modeling is Important" introduces process modeling in general, highlighting how it supports communication and understanding amongst people. It briefly covers how Process Models can aid communication and drive work through the enterprise.

Chapter 3—"Processes" provides a quick introduction to BPMN Process concepts, covering Orchestration, Choreography and Collaboration concepts.

Chapter 4—"Modeling Approaches & Architecture" introduces some of the potential approaches to modeling with BPMN.

Chapter 5—"A Scenario-Based Introduction to BPMN" provides an easy to follow introduction to BPMN modeling. It starts with a simple, easily recognized situation and then builds up on that base, slowly introducing and explaining BPMN functionality to support the evolving behavioral complexity.

Part II Chapter 6—BPMN Reference Section Introduction provides a short preface, explaining the *tokens* that we use to demonstrate the behavior associated with each BPMN element.

Chapter 7—Activities explores Tasks, Sub-Processes and Process Levels in general. It then goes on to discuss the special issues affecting Sub-Processes.

Chapter 8—Events provides detailed explanations of all the Start, Intermediate and End Events. It goes through each one in turn describing the behavior of each element.

Chapter 9—Gateways investigates the role of Gateways in BPMN modeling (points where control is required to split and merge paths), going through the precise behavior associated with each type.

Chapter 10—Swimlanes sets out the precise semantics and rules associated with Pools and Lanes.

Chapter 11—Artifacts discusses how to represent Data, Documents and other things not directly covered with the core process flow diagram objects.

Chapter 12—Connectors explores the meaning associated with Sequence Flow, Message Flow and Annotations.

Chapter 13—Advanced Concepts provides explanations of The Life-Cycle of an Activity, Compensation and Transactions, and Ad Hoc Processes.

Appendices provide a more detailed examination of:

o   Process Execution Environments (BPM Suites and Workflow).

o   Techniques for Process Architecture—a short discussion of some of the available approaches.

o   A collection of BPMN *best practices*.

o   BPMN Directions—discusses the likely direction of the BPMN specification, exploring some of the functionality expected in BPMN 2.0 and subsequent revisions.

Afterword provided by Prof. Michael zur Muehlin discusses some of the uses of Process Models and, through the use of BPMN, how to avoid the mistakes of the past.

Glossary and Index

Typographical Conventions

In this book, we have used the following styles to distinguish BPMN elements over ordinary English. However, these conventions are not used in tables or section headings where no distinction is necessary.

Bookman Old Style - 10.5 pt.:	Standard text
Indented Italics:	*Scenarios*
Initial Capitals:	BPMN Elements
Lower case italics:	*Important BPMN concepts*
Underlined:	General emphasis
Calibri – 10.5 pt. Hanging Indent Italics:	*Key Points and Best Practices*
Calibri – 10.5 pt. Indent (No Italics):	Exercises

Chapter 2.   The Importance of Modeling

Abstract: *This chapter describes the role of Process Modeling in general—both as an aid to communication and also to drive the way in which work happens in the modern organization. It then goes on to discuss a little of the history of BPMN.*

All organizations are on a journey—a never ending voyage where the focus is on improving how things are done (however that is measured) for the benefit of shareholders, stakeholders and/or profit. This notion is at the heart of Business Process Management (BPM); a way of thinking, a management philosophy centered on improving the operational processes of the organization.

The longer an organization has been traveling down this path, the more mature its processes; the more repeatable and scalable its operations and the better its overall business performance. Indeed, management literature is full of examples of firms that have been on this road for some time—Dell, General Electric, Toyota, Nokia, Cisco, Federal Express to name just a few.

Wherever one looks, it is easy to find any number of articles or books that direct firms to engage in operational innovation (with the objective of overwhelming the competition). And yet, all of these examples have one thing in common—an underlying emphasis on understanding the business processes of the firm in order to improve them. One could argue that this is a fundamental principle of management discipline.

Around the world, in virtually every firm and organization, people are struggling to communicate with each other on how to best organize work. They are exploring questions such as:

- Which steps are *really* necessary?
- Who should do them?
- Should they be kept in house or outsourced?
- How they should be done?
- What capabilities are needed?
- What results do we expect and how will they be monitored?

While the answers to these questions are always situation specific, without the backdrop of a commonly agreed description of the business process in question, such answers are often vague and wooly.

Process Models Aid Communication

Competitors bring out new products, customers demand faster turnaround times and lower prices, regulations change. Every time an organizational program kicks off to address these sorts of challenges, people find themselves building business process models to illustrate the flow of work and related activity (see Figure 2-1).

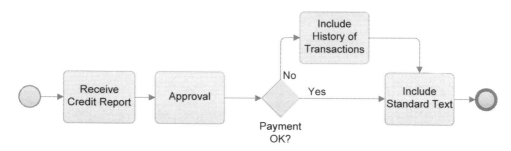

Figure 2-1—A sample BPMN Process

People generally use these models to underpin their conversations, supporting communication and understanding, acting as a backdrop for virtually all improvement programs. Such models often form the basis of a comprehensive business reference, detailing how the entire operation fits together. They feature in training materials and act as a basis for sharing best practice inside the firm.

As depicted in Figure 2-2, process models are normally created (discovered or captured) by looking into the business operations as they stand. Potential inputs here are the goals, strategy and rules (or regulations) of the organization. Some sort of Analysis takes place before Redesign.

Organizations can choose from many sophisticated methodologies for capturing and designing process models to fit their purpose. This book does not aim to provide such a methodology, but will provide a basis for understanding the resulting models.

Up until this point, the assumption is that humans are the primary consumers of these models. As we will see later on, these processes can also act as primary inputs to a business support environment.

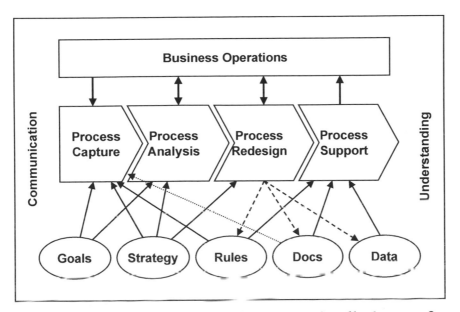

Figure 2-2—Process Models are important in all phases of organizational change

Initially, these models drive communication with work colleagues *inside* the organization, helping them form a shared understanding. In a small organization, this is relatively easy to do since employees tend to share a common culture and a shared set of values. But in a larger organization, especially where employees a spread across several physically disparate locations, achieving a common agreed interpretation of what the words really mean is often difficult.

But when sharing process models with suppliers, customers and/or partners—i.e., up and down the value chain, this issue interpretation issue is exacerbated. The participants no longer have the cultural references that help anchor the meaning to the diagram.

Key Point: *Without a rigorous way of describing business processes, the interpretation of any given model is always up to the reader (not the modeler), which can defeat the purpose.*

Process models also provide the framework within which metrics have meaning. For example, without some notion of business process, concepts such as end-to-end cycle time and activity costs would have no reference points.

Process Models That Drive Work

But having built those models, some realize that it is also possible to use them to drive the work itself. Notice that Figure 2-2 above shows how Process Redesign feeds into Process Support. Along with the Data, Documents and Rules, the Process Model is now the supporting the operations of the business.

Interpreted by sophisticated software systems (BPM Suites or Workflow products), *executable* process models carry the instructions for how work should happen, who should do it, escalation conditions if it is not done in time, links to other systems, etc. The products move work around the organization, ensuring the correct performance of critical steps and that work items do not fall through the cracks.

If the work needs to change then—instead of writing new computer programs (the old approach)—just change the supporting models and the behavior of the organization will adapt correspondingly.

These process-driven software environments are becoming more popular as they provide a direct method of translating strategic and tactical intent into operational processes. They provide the plumbing for the long journey of organizational transformation. In a many different ways, they enable the entire organization to become far more agile than would otherwise be the case. For a more detailed discussion on Process Support and Process Execution in general see the Appendices section "Process Execution Environments" on page 193.[3]

The essential factor here is that process models require more rigor if they are to support this executable behavior (rather than relying on human interpretation). The problem is that, without precision and structure, the more you look at "boxes and arrows," the less they mean. In order for a model to communicate real substance (to the reader or a computer system) the boxes and arrows have to stand for something.

Key Point: *The reality is that, when it comes to modeling the multi-faceted world of work, all business process models need a certain degree of rigor. Otherwise, they are meaningless. This is especially true where the model is designed for interpretation by computers.*

---

[3] See also *Mastering BPM--The Practitioners Guide* by Derek Miers. This book provides a far more extensive discussion on the issues associated with executing Process Models in a BPM Suite.

And that is what the Business Process Modeling Notation (BPMN) is all about. It provides a standard way of representing business processes for both high-level descriptive purposes and for detailed, rigorous process-driven software environments.

Process Modeling in BPMN

In BPMN, a "Business Process" involves capturing an ordered sequence of business activities and supporting information. Modeling a Business Process involves representing how a business pursues its overarching objectives; the objectives themselves are important, but at this point are not captured in the notation. With BPMN, only the processes are modeled.

In developing BPMN, we perceived that there were different levels of process modeling:

- **Process Maps**—simple flow-charts of the activities; a flow diagram without a lot of detail other than the names of the activities and perhaps the broad decision *conditions*.
- **Process Descriptions**—provide more extensive information on the process, such as the people involved in performing the process (roles), the data, information and so forth.
- **Process Models**—detailed flow-charts encompassing sufficient information such that the process is amenable to analysis and simulation. Moreover, this more detailed style of model would also enable either direct execution of the model or import into other tools that could execute that process (with further work).

BPMN covers all these types of models and supports each level of detail. As such, BPMN is a flow chart-based notation for defining business processes from the simple (for example see Figure 2-1 on page 20) to the more complex and sophisticated models required to support process execution.

Key Point: *BPMN is capable of representing many different levels of details and different sorts of diagrams for different purposes.*

The History and Objectives of BPMN

In 2001 BPMI.org[4] began developing BPML (Business Process Modeling Language, an XML process execution language) and realized there was a need for a graphical representation. The indi-

---

[4] Business Process Management Initiative

viduals and vendors involved at the time decided a notation was required that was oriented toward the needs of a business user—i.e. not a notation that directly (canonically) represented the precise execution language under development. This would mean that a translation was needed from the business-oriented notation to the technical execution language. BPML was later replaced by BPEL as the target execution language.

The Notation Working Group (who originally created BPMN within BPMI.org) formed in August 2001. It was composed of 35 modeling companies, organizations, and individuals who between them brought a wide range of perspectives. This Group developed BPMN 1.0.

When we started the development of BPMN there were—and there still are—a wide range of process modeling notations, delivered using different tools, and used within a wide variety of methodologies.

The interesting thing about BPMN was the large number of vendors that came together with the shared objective—to consolidate the underlying principles of process modeling. Their aim was to agree on a single notation (representation) that other tools and users might adopt. Thus, BPMN was not a lofty academic exercise, but rather a practical solution for both process modeling tool vendors and the users of process modeling tools.

The reasoning was that this approach would help end-users, giving them a single, agreed notation. This would enable consistent training, using any number of tools. Companies would not have to retrain every time they bought a new tool or hired people who had studied other tools and notations. In short, it made skills transferable.

Another objective of BPMN was that it would provide a mechanism to generate executable processes—initially in BPML (later substituted with BPEL). Thus, BPMN provides a mapping from "valid" BPMN diagrams to BPEL, such that an engine can execute the process. This does not mean that every BPMN process model is executable, but for those processes intended for execution, BPMN provides the mechanisms to go from original design through to execution. This traceability was part of the original goal for the development of BPMN.

Key Point: *BPMN had two contradictory objectives—to provide an easy to use process modeling notation, accessible to business users; and provide facilities to translate models into an executable form such as BPEL.*

In May 2004, the BPMN 1.0 specification was released to the public. Since then, over 50 companies have developed implementations of the standard. In February 2006 the BPMN 1.0 specification was adopted as an OMG standard (after BPMI.org was folded into the OMG).

Note that the Notation Working Group did not set out to specify an agreed storage mechanism (serialization) for BPMN. This is both a blessing and a curse—it allowed vendors to adopt the notation without having to change their own internal storage formats (a contributing factor to the widespread adoption of the standard). But it also meant that diagram files were not portable between modeling tools.

Key Point: *BPMN did not originally specify a storage format, enabling a wider cross section of vendors to adopt the standard, yet constraining portability of models.*

In February 2008, the OMG released the final BPMN 1.1, which is available for public download (see www.bpmn.org). Most of the changes in version 1.1 clarified the specification document itself, making the meaning more explicit.

However, a few graphical changes were made to BPMN in version 1.1 (all covered in this book). Where changes have occurred, we have highlighted them.

The OMG will soon release BPMN 1.2. This version does not include any significant graphical changes; modifications were merely editorial (i.e. cleaning up the language of the specification itself).

BPMN 2.0 is currently in development and will deliver a major step forward in the capabilities of BPMN. This new version is unlikely to surface until the middle of 2009 at the earliest. For a more extensive discussion on the future of BPMN and the likely facilities of BPMN 2.0 see the Appendix "BPMN Directions" on page 199.

Chapter 3.   Processes

Abstract: *The purpose of this chapter is to explore the various definitions of the term Process before going on to introduce a BPMN diagram, pointing to the key elements presented. It then goes on to discuss the different categories of Processes that BPMN is starting to support (Orchestration, Choreography and Collaboration).*

There are a great many Business Process definitions. Indeed, the notion of a Business Process is an abstract notion at best. In our workshops we often ask people to write down their own definition and are continually amazed at the breadth of the answers we receive. Examples proffered have included:

- A sequence of activities performed on one or more inputs to deliver an output.
- A systematic set of activities that take a "business event" to a successful outcome.
- A collection of business activities that create value for a customer.
- A number of roles collaborating and interacting to achieve a goal.
- An organized collection of business behaviors that satisfy a defined business purpose, performing according to specified targets.
- Just the way things get done around here.

The current Wikipedia definition is, "A business process or business method is a collection of interrelated tasks, which accomplish a particular goal."

The problem, in coming up with a definition for the term Process, is that there are so many of them (definitions)—everyone has a subtly different interpretation. Moreover, we all use the same word and often do not realize that we may mean different things.

So while all these definitions have their merits, we need to settle on one for the purposes of this book. In BPMN a Process represents what an organization does—its work—in order to accomplish a specific purpose or objective. In the bulleted list above, the second and third definitions are probably closest.

Within an organization, there are many types of Processes both in terms of their purpose and how they are performed. Most Processes will require some type of input (either electronic or physical), use and/or consume resources, and produce some type of output (either electronic or physical). Most organizations perform hundreds or thousands of different processes in the course of providing value to customers, staff, or satisfying regulations.

Some processes are formal, repeatable, well-structured, and may even be automated. We often refer to these types of processes as "Procedures." Examples include:

- Healthcare claims processing
- Creating a new account
- Banking transactions
- Expense claims processing

Other processes are informal, very flexible, unpredictable (highly variable), and hard to define or repeat. We sometimes refer to these types of processes as "Practices." Examples include:

- Writing a user manual
- Developing a sales strategy
- Preparing a conference agenda
- Running a consulting engagement

BPMN uses a set of specialized graphical elements to depict a Process and how it is performed (see Figure 3-1). The main elements of a BPMN Process are the *"flow objects"* (Activities—see page 67; Events—see page 85; and Gateways—see page 133), and Sequence Flow (see page 169).

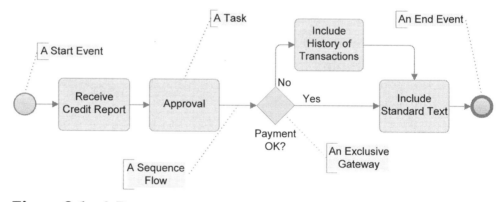

Figure 3-1—A Process

Key Point: *Flow objects (Activities, Events Gateways and Sequence Flow) are the main elements that define the underlying structure and behavior of the Process.*

Modelers often add further graphical elements to explain the Process structure and to provide clarifying details. For example, Data Objects (see page 163) show how data is used with the Process. Other Artifacts such as Groups (see page 164) or Text Annotations (see page 167) help organize or document details of the Process. Lanes can partition the elements by role (or other criteria—see page 159).

Key Point: *Data Objects, Artifacts and Lanes provide further detail, describing the performance or behavior of the Process, but they do not significantly modify the underlying structure (as defined by the flow objects and Sequence Flow).*

Categories of Processes

Since its inception, BPMN has sought to support three main categories of Processes:

- Orchestration
- Choreography
- Collaboration

These terms have varied, with often conflicting, meanings across the many different business contexts within which they are applied. We have sought to define them for the purposes of BPMN, and then apply them consistently throughout this book. Future versions of BPMN will distinguish more clearly between these types of processes, including robust diagrammatic support for each aspect.

Orchestration

Within BPMN, *orchestration* models tend to imply a single coordinating perspective—i.e., they represent a specific business or organization's view of the process. As such, an *orchestration* Process describes how a single business entity goes about things. Used mainly in the technical community, "Process Orchestration" is often aligned with Web Service languages such as BPEL.

The majority of this book explores *orchestration*-oriented process models. So much so, that we will refer to *orchestrations* simply as Processes. Figure 3-2 presents a simple *orchestration* model

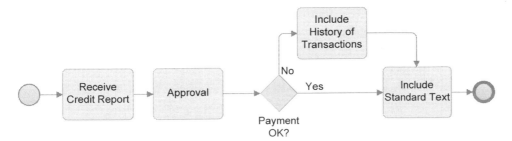

Figure 3-2—A typical BPMN *orchestration*

However, a BPMN diagram may contain more than one *orchestration*. If so, each *orchestration* appears within its own container called a Pool (see page 157). Thus, *orchestrations* (i.e., Processes) are always contained within a Pool. This is an important distinction when understanding the difference between *orchestration* and *choreography*.

Furthermore, the fact that *orchestrations* are contained within a Pool indicates that they consist of process elements that exist together within a well-defined context, or locus of control. An *orchestration* model executed by a BPM Suite certainly fits this description, but it also applies to situations that are not part of a semi-automated system. A consequence of the "well-defined context" for an *orchestration* is that any data is available to all elements of the model.

Choreography

A *choreography* process model is a definition of the expected behavior (a type of procedural contract or protocol) between interacting *participants*. These *participants* could be general business roles (e.g. a shipper) or are a specific business entity (e.g. FedEx as the shipper).

Like the definition of a ballet, a *choreography* in BPMN describes the *interactions* of the *participants*. In BPMN, a *choreography* defines the sequence of *interactions* between two or more *participants*. In BPMN, *interactions* are the communication, in the form of *message* exchanges between two *participants*.

A BPMN *choreography* model shares many of the characteristics of an *orchestration* model in that it has a flow chart form. It includes alternative and parallel paths, as well as Sub-Processes. Thus, the *flow objects* (Activities, Events, and Gateway) of *orchestration* models also apply to *choreography* models.

However, there are dramatic differences between *orchestration* and *choreography* models:

- An *orchestration* is contained within a Pool and normally has a well-formed context.
- A *choreography* does not exist within a well-formed context or locus of control. There is no central mechanism that drives or keeps track of a *choreography*. Therefore, there are no shared data available to all the elements of the *choreography*.

BPMN Modeling and Reference Guide

- To place *choreography* within BPMN diagrams is to put them <u>between</u> the Pools.

The first version of BPMN (now 1.1) included some of the concepts that support *choreography* models. And while it is possible to derive the expected behavior of choreography, the elements needed for full definition have yet to be defined. BPMN 2.0 will include full support for *choreography* diagrams (distinct from *orchestration* diagrams).

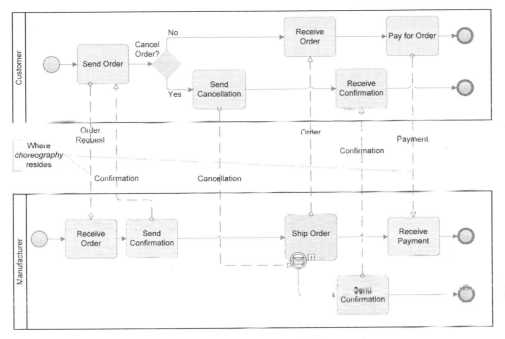

Figure 3-3—Choreography in BPMN (as it is now)

Figure 3-3 above demonstrates the current capabilities for *choreography* definition within BPMN 1.1. The diagram shows two Pools, each containing *orchestrations*. The connectors between the Pools are Message Flow (see page 173). The combination of the Activities and other elements within the Pools and the Message Flow between the Pools defines an implicit *choreography*.

We expect BPMN 2.0 to include an explicit *choreography diagram*. Rather than having to derive the choreography from the message exchange, it will be possible to model it "stand-alone" or place it between the Pools.

Collaboration

Collaboration has a specific meaning in BPMN. Where a *choreography* defines the ordered set (a protocol) of *interactions* between *participants*, a *collaboration* simply shows the *participants* and their *interactions*. A *collaboration* may also <u>contain</u> a *choreography* (when it is available in BPMN) and one or more *orchestrations*.

To be more specific, a *collaboration* is any BPMN diagram that contains two or more *participants* as shown by Pools. The Pools have Message Flow between them. Any of the Pools may contain an *orchestration* (a Process), but they are not required.

Figure 3-4 shows an example *collaboration* diagram. It contains two Pools and Message Flow between them. Other *collaboration* diagrams could show *orchestrations* within the Pools (as in Figure 3-3, above).

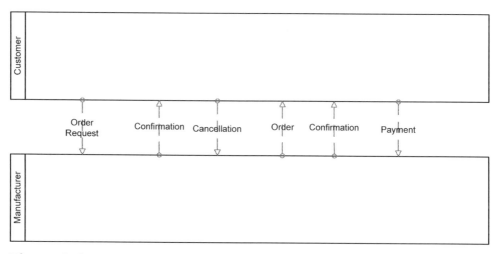

Figure 3-4—An example of a *collaboration* in BPMN

Chapter 4.   Modeling Issues

Abstract: *The purpose of this chapter is to discuss some of the issues associated with Process modeling in general, and to identify some of the challenges in dealing with these issues. The associated Appendix (Techniques for Process Architecture on page 195) discusses several of the available approaches that can help the modeler identify an appropriate Process Architecture.[5]*

"All Models are Wrong, Some are Useful"

This quotation, variously attributed to Edwards Deming but actually originating from the lesser-known Charles Box,[6] describes the predicament in which modelers find themselves. There are usually a great many ways of modeling a desired behavior, at any number of levels of precision.

Key Point: *Many people assume that there is always a correct model (and that somehow other models are wrong) however, there is seldom only one correct model. On the other hand, models might be <u>invalid</u> (in that they incorrectly use a given notation).*

Moreover, there is often far more potential detail to capture than is necessary. If we were to model how one goes about making a cup of tea, then a single Activity might be sufficient. Alternatively, one could describe the need to first boil the water, place a tea bag in a cup and optionally add milk. But what if we liked to brew the tea for several people using a teapot and tea leaves, or should we include the steps involved in filling the kettle, or adding sugar. The modeler is always making decisions about what to include and what leave out. So one needs to maintain a perspective about the uses of the model and who will interpret it.

If the audiences (those who will read and interpret the model) are not interested in the fine detail, then do not include it in the model. In other situations, such as where the model will support execution on a BPM Suite or where simulation is the objective, then significant detail is normally required.

---

[5] While this is outside the scope of the BPMN standard itself, this is of interest to modelers as they tend to assume that somehow BPMN will help them decide on what processes exist for a given domain.

[6] Charles Box first used it as a heading in a book chapter in 1979—Citation: Box, G.E.P., *Robustness in the Strategy of Scientific Model Building*, in Robustness in Statistics, R.L. Launer and G.N. Wilkinson, Editors. 1979, Academic Press: New York.

At the beginning of one of our workshops, we go through a very simple exercise. We ask delegates to brainstorm all the things that they would want represent on process models. It is not long before we have filled a couple of white boards—activities, flow, inputs, outputs, responsibilities, costs, locations, quality, rules, interactions, escalation, etc. Asked if they would want all of these dimensions to appear on a single process, delegates suddenly realize it is a question of removing things from the models to make them useful.

Key Point: *The modeler is constantly making modeling decisions about the purpose of the model and the intended audience.*[7]

An anecdotal story drives home the point. During the days of Business Process Reengineering (BPR was sometimes referred to as Bigger People Reductions), a major chemicals giant employed one of the leading consulting firms to assist with the reengineering of their North American sales process. After several months of work, a presentation was staged for the main board (as this was a highly important project). On one side of the meeting room was an eighty foot flow diagram (the As Is model). On the other wall, a sixty foot flow diagram of the To Be process. The then-Chairman allowed the Consultancy Partner to complete his presentation before asking a very simple question. "Is that a good process and if so, please explain why." And therein lay the core of the problem. The detail delivered was wholly inappropriate for the intended audience.

Here are some traits of a good model:[8]

- **Salient**—Since no model can represent everything, it must selectively represent those things that are most relevant to the task at hand.
- **Accurate**—The model should precisely encode the actual state of affairs and not an erroneous or biased view.
- **Complete yet Parsimonious**—The model should be as simple as possible, but no simpler.[9]

---

[7] Some vocal modelers seem to feel that notation should provide only one way of representing any particular problem. But this attitude flies in the face of reality and expecting only one possible model for a given scenario is unrealistic; all models are a compromise. BPMN often provides a range of functionality to facilitate different modelling purposes and styles.

[8] Marshal Clemens of consultancy firm, Idiagram, offers some excellent guidance on the features that models should exhibit. He is not discussing BPMN, but many of the points are still relevant. http://www.idiagram.com/ideas/models.html

[9] Here he is paraphrasing Einstein.

- **Understandable**—Once we perceive the model we must be able to make sense of it; it shouldn't be too complicated or unfamiliar for us to understand.

Clemens goes on to point to some of the evolution and adaptability issues around modeling. "As all models are, to some degree, inaccurate, irrelevant, mistaken, time-sensitive etc., they should be open to recursive revision to reflect new data, our growing understanding, or our evolving needs."

In the end, models need to be useful. Clemens continues, "Usefulness is the sum of the above properties and the degree to which they combine to promote understanding and effective action. It is important to note that the most accurate, or the most complete, or the most elegant model is not necessarily the most useful. All models are incomplete. All models are a compromise. The model maker's art lies in making those shrewd trade offs that will render the model most useful to the problem at hand."

Key Point: *In order to be useful, all models selectively represent some elements of the real world. The modeler excludes different dimensions of the domain (in order to achieve the modeling goals).*

How Many Processes, Where Do They Fit?

The temptation is always to leap straight in and start modeling. Yet a more considered approach normally pays significant dividends.

The real problem is that as people begin to describe how things happen in an area of their organization, they assume that it is all one big process. We often see it in our workshops. Students try to connect everything up together into one amorphous process description that captures every possible permutation.

Key Point: *Very often, it is inordinately difficult to model one "end-to-end" process for a given business problem. And even if it were possible, it is challenging to make that model flexible and adaptable.*

It is usually far better to break up a given domain problem into a number of discrete "chunks," that working together solve the problem. So the issue becomes one of how to come up with the right chunks. But when looking for techniques, one finds remarkably few.

For a wider discussion on the various approaches for organizing, scoping models, see the Appendix "Techniques for Process Architecture" on page 195. Here we outline a set of approaches that, between them, provide a translation from the business strategy level right through to a robust process architecture (independent of the reporting structure of the organization). Potentially, these techniques could extend into a stack of IT services (as part of a Service Oriented Architecture).

The point is that BPMN is "methodology agnostic." Organizations typically have a preferred methodology for capturing and developing their business processes. It is not the role of BPMN to dictate how business process information is collected or how modeling projects are undertaken. Therefore, BPMN supports multiple methodologies (being as simple or complex as it needs to be). It does not specify the level of detail for models—the modeler, modeling tool, or organization makes these decisions. Indeed, as we will see with process modeling in general; usually there exists many different ways of modeling the same situation, with any number of different levels of detail.

Key Point: *BPMN does not provide any advice on how to structure a domain or come up with an appropriate architecture for a given area. Yet it provides capabilities that can support many different methods.*

Dealing with Complexity in BPMN

So as we can see from the above, business processes can become complex—very complex (covered in more depth in the Appendix). However, most developers and readers of process models want a simple, graphical language for depicting Business Processes. In fact, the majority of all process models are simple flow charts (activity boxes, decision diamonds, and the connectors between them). At the same time, modelers need enough flexibility to represent further levels of complexity if they needed.

The objective of most process modeling projects is to document (understand) and analyze an organizations key business processes. Yet these same models can then become the basis for a more detailed set of Process descriptions for other uses. Elaborated and built upon with further detail, they might then become executable (in a BPM Suite or workflow tool).

For example, a rather simplistic model (originally developed for a business model discussion), may end up being adapted for use in establishing appropriate partner relationships (defining the interfaces), which is then further embellished and adapted by both parties to support their respective process execution environments.

Since each company or modeler may want to show different levels or areas of complexity, the notation needs enough flexibility to handle virtually all possible business situations or modeling requirements. But the problem is that such a modeling notation, one that is capable of depicting all business situations, is no longer simple, it is complex.

This issue points to the dynamic tension that exists between the two primary goals of BPMN:

- On the one hand, ease of use for business user and business analyst;
- And on the other, executable processes.

To meet the requirements of the first goal, BPMN is structured with a small set of elements (e.g., Activities, Events, and Gateways) that have distinctive shapes (e.g., rectangle, circle, and diamond). The small set of main elements supports the simplicity and readability of the models.

To meet the requirements of the second goal, the main elements are specialized for specific purposes, each of which carry further information and/or supported with more elements to allow the modeling of the required behavior. In addition, the underlying semantic structure of BPMN must be rigorous, containing information that enables the generation of valid BPEL; or at least set the stage for other tools to complete the development and deployment.[10]

The BPMN specification includes a lot of information and capabilities that make it look complicated. However, it is unlikely that the business analyst or end user needs most of these capabilities (as they relate to the execution semantics). In this book, we will point out the core BPMN elements that should appeal to the Business Analyst, while also providing thorough descriptions of the more advanced BPMN elements.

Key Point: *While the BPMN modeling technique may appear a little daunting to the uninitiated, it is only as complex as it needs to be in order to support both ease of use for the business analyst and end user; and at the same time, enable elaboration of models to support process execution.*

---

[10] With a rigorous definition of the semantics of a BPMN model, some BPM Suites are capable of executing the Process model directly, without further translation to an intermediate language such as BPEL. With the emergence of BPMN 2.0 this capability will be further enhanced as the underlying semantics become yet more rigorous.

Chapter 5.   Scenario-Based BPMN Introduction

Abstract: *This chapter provides the reader with a gradual introduction to the BPMN specification, taking an easily understood scenario and then slowly building upon it, bringing in BPMN functionality within that described context.*

Designed for those coming to BPMN for the first time, it allows them to familiarize themselves with the core features of the Notation without being overwhelmed by the complexity of some of the more esoteric aspects.

Most of the functionality is limited to the "core" set of BPMN elements with which a Business Analyst should be familiar. This concept of the core set is expanded upon in the reference section.

Building out a Process with BPMN

The central scenario used within this chapter revolves around a fictitious organization Mortgage Co. They take applications from potential customers, make an assessment whether or not to offer the mortgage, and then either reject the application or make the offer (see Figure 5-1). [11]

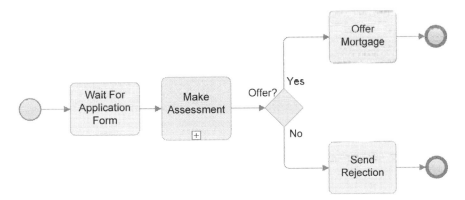

Figure 5-1—The underlying mortgage offer scenario

Clearly, this is a rather simplistic picture of how such a process might operate. But it will suffice in providing the backdrop for us to introduce the functionality of BPMN. Through the remainder of

---

[11] All paragraphs that build on the underlying scenario will share this font style (indented slightly and italics).

this part of the book, we will systematically build on that underlying scenario, embellishing the story and bringing in the appropriate BPMN modeling features to represent the desired behavior.[12]

The Process begins on the left with a Start Event (thin line circle), with two Activities (rounded rectangles) connected to the Start Event with Sequence Flow (the arrows). The first Activity is a Task and the second represents a Sub-Process. Following a *decision*, represented by the diamond (called an Exclusive Gateway), the Process then branches to either "Offer Mortgage" or "Send Rejection" (both represented here as simple Tasks). Both branches lead to an End Event (thick circle).

Start Events represent the places that a Process can *start*, End Events represent different *results*, some of which might be desired and others not. An Exclusive Gateway represents a binary decision—only one *outgoing* Sequence Flow can evaluate to *true*. For the purposes of this model, the three Tasks represent simple "atomic" steps, whereas the *collapsed* Sub-Process has a further level of detail.

More details on the elements introduced are available in the BPMN Reference Section:

Start Events on page 85

- Tasks on page 68.
- Sub-Processes on page 69.
- Exclusive Gateways on page 135.
- End Events on page 123.
- Sequence Flow on page 169.

Setting Timers

Now, let us assume that we want to represent the fact that our potential customer contacted Mortgage Co to ask for a mortgage application form. For the moment, we will not worry about precisely how they contacted the company, but let us assume it was a "message" of some sort. Further, we want to set a clock running to send them a reminder after seven days if Mortgage Co does not receive their application form back (see Figure 5-2).

---

[12] We refer to the graphical elements of BPMN with Initial Capitals. Where an important BPMN concept is referenced (that is not a graphical element), we have used *italics* within the sentence.

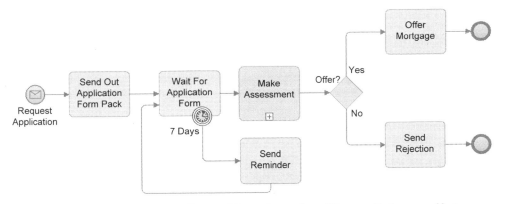

Figure 5-2—A Message Start Event and a Timer Intermediate Event are introduced

The Process now begins with a Message Start Event representing the message received by Mortgage Co who then sends out the application form; a timer is placed on the waiting task to interrupt it and send a reminder before *looping* back again to wait for the application form again.

There are many types of Start Events in BPMN; here we have used a Message Start Event to indicate how this Process begins. Intermediate Events placed on the boundary of a Task means that if the Event fires, then it will interrupt the Task and send the Process down its *outgoing* Sequence Flow. If the Task completes before the Intermediate Event fires, then the Process moves on normally (following the *normal flow* of the Process). The loop is created explicitly with Sequence Flow although, as we will discover later, there are alternatives (i.e., use a Loop Task).

More details on the elements introduced are available in the BPMN Reference Section:

- Message Start Events on page 89.
- Interrupting Activities with Events on page 99.
- Timer Intermediate Events on page 103.
- Looping on page 76.

There is another way to model this scenario using a Sub-Process for the send out application form and wait for the response Figure 5-3.

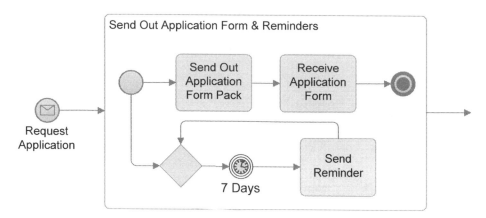

Figure 5-3—Using a Sub-Process to represent the application form and reminders

The Timer Intermediate Event shown in line with the Sequence Flow triggers immediately the Sub-Process begins (the Sub-Process is shown in its *expanded* form). It waits for seven days before that thread of activity moves to the "Send Reminder" Task before looping back to wait for another seven days. When an Intermediate Event is used in line (as in this case), then it can have only one *incoming* and one *outgoing* Sequence Flow. Therefore, merging the *incoming* Sequence Flow before the Timer Intermediate Event requires an Exclusive Gateway. When *merging* Sequence Flow, an Exclusive Gateway immediately passes through any *incoming* Sequence Flow so in this case it serves to clean up the Sequence Flow (but does not represent any sort of delay).

Of course, other *flow objects* (Activities or Gateways) can normally have multiple *incoming* and *outgoing* Sequence Flow. While the Sub-Process could have included a Parallel Gateway to create the split (see Figure 5-4), it is unnecessary as the Sequence Flow does not require control. Figure 5-3 and Figure 5-4 describe exactly the same behavior. A general rule is that Gateways are only required where Sequence Flow requires *control*.

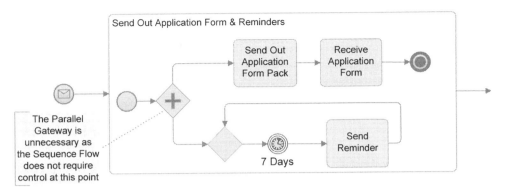

Figure 5-4—Using a Parallel Gateway is unnecessary

The Sub-Process finishes with a Terminate End Event. The Terminate End Event causes the immediate cessation of the Process on its current level (and below) even if there is still ongoing activity. Effectively, it kills off the reminder *loop*.

More details on the elements introduced are available in the BPMN Reference Section:

- Timer Intermediate Events on page 103.
- Terminate End Event on page 128.
- Parallel Gateways on page 143.
- Text Annotations on page 167.

Exercise One

Try modeling this process; it will help ensure that the techniques discussed so far sink in:

> Every weekday morning, the database is backed up and then it is checked to see whether the "Account Defaulter" table has new records. If no new records are found, then the process should check the CRM system to see whether new returns have been filed. If new returns exist, then register all defaulting accounts and customers. If the defaulting client codes have not been previously advised, produce another table of defaulting accounts and send to account management. All of this must be completed by 2:30 pm, if it is not, then an alert should be sent to the supervisor. Once the new defaulting account report has been completed, check the CRM system to see whether new returns have been filed. If new returns have been filed, reconcile with the existing account defaulters table. This must be completed by 4:00 pm otherwise a supervisor should be sent a message.

Looping

So far, the *loop* is expressed using explicit Sequence Flow coming back to an earlier part of the Process. BPMN provides another mechanism to represent this sort of behavior—the Loop Task (see Figure 5-5). A Loop Task has a small semi-circular arrow that curls back upon itself.

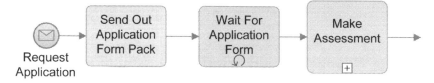

Figure 5-5--A simple Loop Task

It is possible to set BPMN attributes to support sophisticated looping behavior.[13] This is required to support the necessary complexity required by simulation and process execution environments. These aspects are discussed fully in the BPMN Reference Section.

> *Now clearly, it does not make much sense to endlessly loop back to wait for an application form that may never arrive. So after two such reminders, Mortgage Co has decided to cancel the application and archive the details.*

There is another way of setting the loop counter in Figure 5-6. Instead of using a graphically modeled "Set Loop Counter" Task, the "Send Reminder" Task could set an *assignment* at the level of the attributes. Although invisible, an annotation could then highlight its existence.

It is worth noting that the explicit Sequence Flow *loop* <u>cannot</u> cycle back to the Start Event. Indeed, Start Events cannot have *incoming* Sequence Flow. The *loop* can only go back as far the first Task.

---

[13] Looping and other element attributes store information about the Process that is not shown graphically.

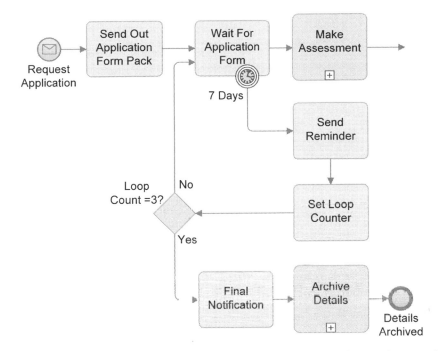

Figure 5-6—A loop counter is set and after two iterations, the details are archived and the Process ends

More details on the elements introduced are available in the BPMN Reference Section:

- Looping on page 76.

Decisions Based On Events

Of course, if the customer never sends back their application form, then the process will never get to the assessment phase. But what if the customer does let Mortgage Co know that they do not wish to proceed with the mortgage? The model in Figure 5-6 does not adequately represent this subtly different scenario.

Now, after sending the application pack, Mortgage Co waits for one of three different things to happen. Either they receive the application (it moves on to the "Make Assessment" Task), or they are notified that the customer does not wish to proceed (in which case "Archive Details"), or after 7 days a reminder is sent (twice before sending a final advice and archiving the details).

While it is possible to model such a scenario using Activities, Sequence Flow and Exclusive Gateways, the model would become very messy and convoluted. There is another way of modeling this situation, making use of an Event-Based Exclusive Gateway (see Figure 5-7).

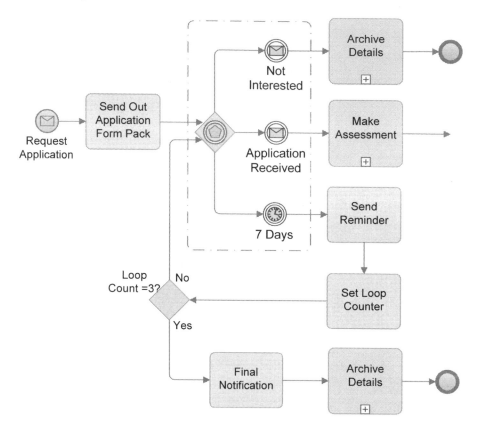

Figure 5-7—Using an Event-Based Exclusive Gateway

The Event-Based Exclusive Gateway (or informally, the Event Gateway) and its following Intermediate Events are regarded as a whole (the dot-dashed line around them is a BPMN Group used for emphasis only). To differentiate it from other Gateways, the Event Gateway reuses the Multiple Intermediate Event marker in the center of the diamond. Effectively, the Gateway waits for <u>one</u> the subsequent Events to occur. Either a *message* is received (Message Intermediate Event) indicating the customer is "Not Interested" or the "Application Received" Message Intermediate Event occurs (and the Process can progress), or the *timer* goes off and the reminder *loop* is initiated. Another Sub-Process could represent the reminder *loop*.

Notice that the "Archive Details" *collapsed* Sub-Process appears twice on the diagram. This Sub-Process is designed as a *reusable* Sub-Process. It might appear in other Processes outside the scope of this. Effectively, it represents a stand-alone Process referenced

BPMN Modeling and Reference Guide

by this one. Of course, one could reorganize the diagram to use only one Activity on this model.

More details on each element introduced are available in the BPMN Reference Section:

- Event-Based Exclusive Gateways on page 140.
- Message Intermediate Events on page 107.
- Groups on page 164.
- Multiple Intermediate Events on page 123.

Meeting SLAs

Now let us assume that Mortgage Co receives the application form back and they have decided to institute a Service Level Agreement with their customers. They are now promising to respond with an offer or rejection within 14 days from the date of receipt of an application form. In support of this, the Process should alert the manager after 10 days if it has not completed, and then every day thereafter. Also, they need to archive the details if the decision was to reject the application (before the end of the Process).

Thinking about the alert, the first temptation is probably to use a Sub-Process and then attach a Timer Intermediate Event to its border to create the alert (similar to Figure 5-2 on page 41). The problem with this approach is that it will *interrupt* the work of the Sub-Process, and a *loop* back to the beginning would cause the work to start again (not the desired behavior). The work should not stop just to raise an alert to the manager. Figure 5-8 shows one approach to solving this problem.

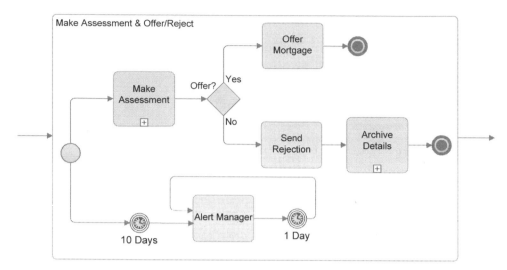

Figure 5-8—One approach to the non-interrupt alert problem

A separate Process *path* (or *thread*) with a Timer Intermediate Event linked to the Start Event of the Sub-Process is one approach to create a non-interrupting alert. The *timer* kicks in after 10 days if the work of the other thread has not finished—if that work is completed, then one or other of the Terminate End Events will kill off the *timer*. Effectively, a *race condition* occurs between these two strands of the process. Once the "Alert Manager" Task has occurred, it waits another day before looping back.

Representing Roles in Processes

The "Alert Manger" Task in Figure 5-8 above seems to imply that the manager receives a *message*. However, *messages* have a special importance in BPMN. Message Flow can only move between separate *participants* in a business-to-business situation. Each *participant* operates a separate Process represented by Pools. Message Flow coordinates the Processes of each *participant*.

Essentially, a Process exists within a single Pool. Labeled boxes display the Pool; they also have square corners as opposed to Tasks and Sub-Processes, which have rounded corners. BPMN uses Pools when representing the interaction between an organization and *participants* outside of its control. Within a company, a single Pool covers its own internal operations—it is only when it interacts with external *participants* that additional Pools are required.[14]

---

[14] Separate Pools might be used where an organization had several independent business units that were collaborating. In such a situation, each business unit would not

For example, in our Mortgage Co, the Credit Agency (and the Customer) would have a separate Pool (assuming one was trying to represent the interactions between the parties).

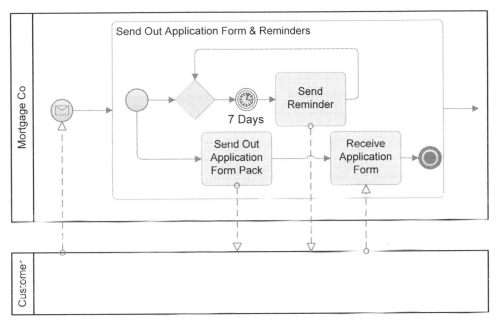

Figure 5-9—Representing the customer in a separate Pool

Message Flow cannot communicate between Tasks inside a single Pool—that is what Sequence Flow and *data flow* (as we shall see below) does. It moves the Process from one Activity to another. In this example (see Figure 5-9) the "Customer" Pool is shown interacting with a fragment of the "Mortgage Co" Process.

Mortgage Co does do not know the Customer's internal Process. Hence, the representation for the Customer is a "Black Box Pool." Within the Mortgage Co's Pool, the Message Start Event receives an *incoming message* from the Customer, which triggers the Sub-Process. A race condition starts between the two threads of the Sub-Process.

Two of the Tasks in the Sub-Process are Send types of Tasks, while the third is a Receive Task. In BPMN 1.1, there is no standard graphical way to differentiate Send and Receive Tasks. Their type is implied by the direction of the Message Flow and stored as attributes.

necessarily know the internal operations of the others, yet would need to indentify the interfaces between them.

Further details on each element introduced are available in the BPMN Reference Section:

- Message Flow on page 173.
- Pools on page 157.
- Lanes on page 159.
- Send and Receive Tasks on page 68

Exercise 2

Try this exercise.

> The Customer Service Representative sends a Mortgage offer to the customer and waits for a reply. If the customer calls or writes back declining the mortgage, the case details are updated and the work is archived prior to cancellation. If the customer sends back the completed offer documents and attaches all prerequisite documents then the case is moved to administration for completion. If all pre-requisite documents are not provided a message is generated to the customer requesting outstanding documents. If no answer is received after 2 weeks, the case details are updated prior to archive and cancellation. [15]

Modeling Data and Documents

> *Mortgage Co handles a lot of documents. They come from lots of different sources—the "Surveyors Report," the "Credit Report," the "Title Search" and the "Application Form." In the context of the Processes of the firm, the documents move through various states as the employees carry out their work. The documents are handled, scanned, sorted, annotated, versioned, archived, etc. Images are linked to customer records, with employees transposing some of their content into data fields for the company's information systems.*

Clearly, there is a need to understand how these data and documents are manipulated within a given process. For example, in Figure 5-10, the "Rejection Letter" and "Assessment" Documents are represented by Data Objects. Data Objects are the Artifacts of the Process. They do not move along with the Process flow, but act as inputs and outputs of Tasks.

---

[15] Example answers to these Exercises will be made available online at http://www.bpmnreferenceguide.com/

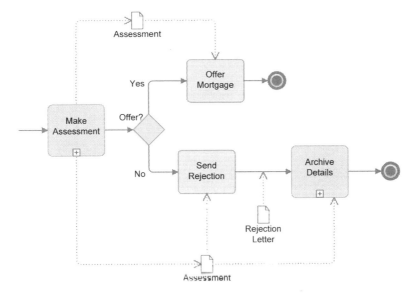

Figure 5-10—Representing documents in the Process

Data Objects exist outside of the Sequence Flow of the Process, but they are available to all *flow objects* in a given Process *instance*. *Data flow* passes information into or out of an Activity. Of course, the implementation mechanism used in any given system is going be specific to the platform used to support the process.

Figure 5-10 above demonstrates two different ways of showing *data flow*. The "Assessment" Data Object is *output* from the "Make Assessment" Sub-Process using an Association connector. The "Assessment" Data Object is also *input* to the "Archive Details" Sub Process. The arrowheads on the Association indicate the direction of the *data flow*.

The "Rejection Letter" Data Object is attached to the Sequence Flow between "Send Rejection" and "Archive Details." This is really a sort of shorthand used when the *data flow* is between two Activities follow each other.

Another subtle implication of the *incoming data flow* is that it tells the reader that these Data Objects must be available in order for the Tasks to start. For example, when the Sequence Flow arrives at the "Send Rejection" Task, it sets the *state* of the Activity to *ready*. It is ready to begin, but it cannot start until all of its inputs (the "Assessment" Data Object) are available. [16]

---

[16] Actually, it is technically possible to set the underlying attributes of the Activity to allow it to start and have updated Data Objects arrive while the Activity is in progress.

More details on each of the elements introduced are available in the BPMN Reference Section:

- Data Objects on page 163.
- Association on page 174.
- Superficial discussion of The Life-Cycle of an Activity on page 181.

Coordinating Parallel Threads of Activity

Coming back to the processes of Mortgage Co, we have so far avoided a core component of their business—making assessments about mortgages and their viability.

The "Make Assessment" Sub-Process is where the real work of the Process happens. Contained within that Activity are a number of Sub-Processes that need to occur in parallel; the credit check, property title search and property survey.

The problem is that Mortgage Co also needs to keep its costs down and at the same time respond as quickly as possible to customer requests. So they have teams that need to do things in parallel and yet still have the ability to communicate with the other teams should one team identify a problem that would invalidate the mortgage application. In the past, they have tried using email for this, but have found it inefficient and prone to cases slipping through the cracks.

While the detail of each of these Sub-Processes is not so important at this point, the key issue to observe is that a bad result in either of these areas will invalidate the mortgage (or at least imply that work in the other areas should halt).

Of course, a good result in any one of these areas means that work can start immediately on preparing the Mortgage offer documents, but that work needs to halt should a negative result come back from one of the other areas. In this way Mortgage Co can enable, as much as possible, efficiency and at the same time reduce the cycle time of the process.

There is another way of handling communication in BPMN. Instead of a directed *message* (that has to go to a particular external *participant*), or Sequence Flow (that cannot cross a Pool or Sub-Process boundary); *Signals* offer a general inter-process communication capability. They can operate within a Process or between Pools and they can cross Process boundaries—think of them like a signal flare or fire siren. They are not directed a specific recipient, instead all who are interested can look/listen and detect the *signal* and then act appropriately.

The Signal Intermediate Events have two distinct modes of operation. They either send *signals* or listen for them. In Figure 5-11 below, the Signal Intermediate Events are all set to listen (they are all in the bottom Sub-Process "Prepare Offer Letter"). That is, they *catch* the Signal broadcast by the Signal End Events. All the Signal End Events send *signals*—that is they *throw* the *signal*.

Where Intermediate Events *catch* the *trigger* shown in the center is white (as in a Start Event); where they *throw*, the center is solid (like an End Event).

Of course, a Signal Intermediate Event can also *throw* (in which case it would have two concentric thin lines with a solid triangle in the center).

Indeed, all *trigger* Events (Start, Intermediate, and End), either *throw* or *catch*. This is inherent to what Events really are.

All Start Events *catch*—that is, that they can only receive *incoming triggers*. It does not make sense for a Start Event to "send," it responds to an Event that happens. Somehow, it is detected and that is what triggers the Event. The markers for all Start Events are white-filled.

All End Events *throw*—they can only fire *triggers* for other Events to *catch*. End Events cannot detect things that happen (what would they do with them, they are at the end?). Instead, they can create Events to which others respond. The markers for End Events are black-filled.

Depending on the sort of Intermediate Event and its contextual usage, the Event either *throws* or *catches* (or both) the *trigger*. Some Intermediate Events always come in pairs; others operate independently. The *catch* Intermediate Event markers are white-filled and the *throw* Intermediate Event markers are black-filled.

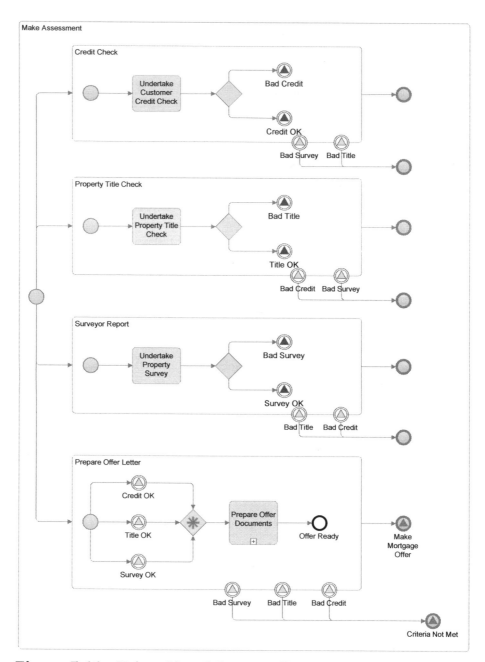

Figure 5-11—Using Signal Intermediate Events to communicate

In Figure 5-11 above, *catch* Signal Intermediate Events are set to capture the *signals* broadcast by the End Events of the first three Sub-Processes (the "Credit OK," "Title OK" or "Survey OK" results). If a "Bad Survey," "Bad Credit" or "Bad Title" End Event occurs, it will trigger one of the Intermediate Events attached to each of the boundaries of the other Sub-Processes, thereby interrupting all of the work going on there.

The "Prepare Offer Letter" Sub-Process starts along with the other three Sub-Processes, but then waits for any one of these *signals* to occur. As soon as one of them happens (detected by the Signal Intermediate Event), it moves the Process on to the Complex Gateway (diamond with a bold asterisk at its center). This Complex Gateway is used to merge the Sequence Flow from these three Intermediate Events.

A Complex Gateway enables the modeler to capture behavior that does not exist in the other Gateways. Think of it as a warning that here the system is likely to drop into complex rules or code. In this case, the "Prepare Offer Documents" Sub-Process can start upon detection of any of the three *signals*. But as other *signals* are detected, a new *instance* of the Sub-process is not required. A normal Exclusive Gateway would result in duplicate process *instances* as each new Event happened.

If a "Bad Survey," "Bad Title" or "Bad Credit" Signal Intermediate Event fires, then the "Prepare Offer Letter" Sub-Process is also interrupted leading it to fire a "Criteria Not Met" Signal End Event. Assuming none of those things happen, the entire "Make Assessment" Sub-Process will complete normally with a "Make Mortgage Offer" Signal End Event.

The "Make Assessment" Sub-Process (*expanded* in Figure 5-11 above, but *collapsed* again in Figure 5-12), will send one of the two possible *signals* back to the *parent* Process: "Make Mortgage Offer" or "Criteria Not Met."

The decision (using an Event-Base Gateway) to offer the mortgage now operates in parallel to the "Make Assessment" Sub-Process. It is waiting for either the "Make Mortgage Offer" or the "Criteria Not Met" *signal* (*thrown* by the Sub-Process). If the Event-Based Gateway was inline, after the "Make Assessment" Sub-Process, then the *signals* in the Sub-Process would fire before the *parent* was ready for them (in which case they are ignored). Notice also that the "Make Assessment" Sub-Process goes to a None End Event— that thread will finish without affecting either of the two branches from the "Offer?" Event-Based Gateway.[17]

---

[17] Technically, the *signals* fire at the end of the sub-process which is also the same time that the Event Gateway fires, so the *signal* would probably be detected. This model is drawn in parallel to ensure the required behavior occurs.

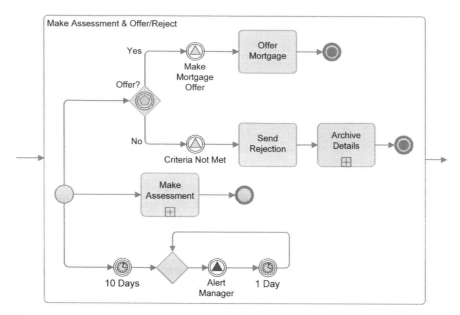

Figure 5-12—A revised "Make Assessment & Offer/Reject" Sub-Process

Here the *signals* communicate between different levels of the Process (between Sub-Processes and the *parent* Process). Without the use of a *signal*, coordination would rely on Process data (and an Exclusive Gateway). In the end, it is a matter of personal choice—i.e. a modeling decision.

More details on each of the elements introduced are available in the BPMN Reference Section:

- Signal Intermediate Event on page 110.
- Intermediate Event Behavior on page 98.
- End Events on page 123.
- Signal End Event on page 127.
- Complex Gateway Merging Behavior on page 154.
- Exclusive Gateway Merging Behavior on page 138.

Exercise 3

Another brainteaser, but think carefully about all the things covered in the book thus far:

> In November of each year, the Coordination Unit at the Town Planning Authority drafts a schedule of meetings for the next calendar year and adds draft dates to all calendars. The Support Officer then checks the dates and suggests modifications. The Coordination Unit then rechecks all dates and look for potential conflicts. The final schedule of meeting dates is sent to all the independent Committee Members by email,

who then check their diaries and advise the Coordination Unit of any conflicts. Once the dates have been finalized by the Coordination Unit, the Support Officer updates all group calendars and creates meeting folders for each meeting and ensures all appropriate documents are uploaded to system. Committee Members are advised a week before each meeting to read all related documents. The Committee Members hold their meeting, and the Support Office then produces minutes including any Action Points for each Committee Member. Within 5 working days the Coordination Unit must conduct a QA check on the minutes which are then sent to all Committee Members. The Support Officer then updates all departmental records.

Another Approach to Escalation

Returning to the non-interrupting alert needed (for the manager discussed for the model in Figure 5 8), it is unlikely that the Manager works for an external business entity, so the Task is not a Send Task.

Figure 5-12 above also uses a Signal Intermediate Event to initiate (*throw*) the interaction with the Manager role. In Figure 5-13, a corresponding Signal Intermediate Event exists in the Manager Lane to listen for such an escalation—i.e., it is waiting to *catch*. In this case, the Signal Intermediate Event supports communication at the same level within a single Pool but across two Lanes.

Figure 5-13 provides yet another alternative approach to the non-interrupt alert problem. It also provides an overview of the Process developed so far.

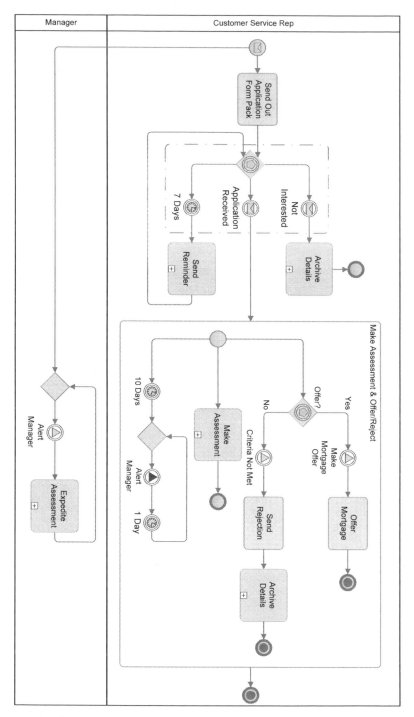

Figure 5-13—The complete Process employing two Lanes to represent the customer service representative and the manager, making use of Signal Events and to coordinate the offer decision with the Sub-Processes of Figure 5-11

BPMN Modeling and Reference Guide

More Than One Right Answer

Just like decisions taken by the modeler (what detail to include and how to present it), decisions taken within a Process do not always have just one correct answer.

Consider Mortgage Co as it compiles the offer documents for its customers. Depending on the mortgage applied for, different documents are required. So a generic mortgage application Process needs mechanisms to differentiate which sub-set of documents to include—let us assume a main proposal plus any number of supplements.

The precise detail of each rule is not our concern here, but providing a Process backdrop for those decisions is not easy if the modeler is restricted to Exclusive Gateways. Process models would become inordinately complex and difficult to follow.

BPMN provides a couple of mechanisms to handle this sort of challenge. The Inclusive Gateway allows for decisions, where all *outgoing* Sequence Flow *conditions* that evaluate to *true* are activated. This is in stark contrast to the Exclusive Gateway where only the first *condition* that evaluates to *true* is activates (all others are ignored).

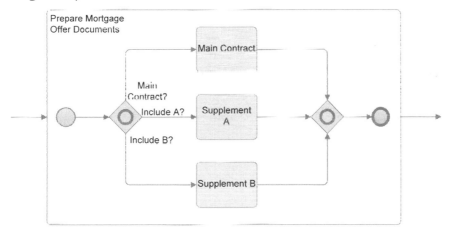

Figure 5-14—Dealing with decisions that have more than one right answer

The *splitting* Inclusive Gateway has a circle at its center to indicate that each *outgoing* Sequence Flow is evaluated. If it returns a *true* value, then the Sequence Flow is activated.

The other approach is to use Conditional Sequence Flow (see Figure 5-15). Each Conditional Sequence Flow has a mini-diamond at the point it leaves and Activity. Each is evaluated in turn and if it returns a *true* value then the Sequence Flow is activated.

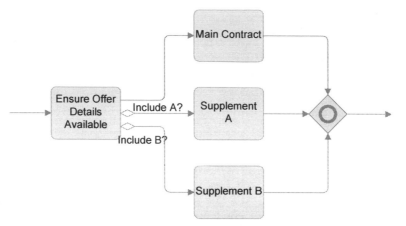

Figure 5-15—Using Conditional Sequence Flow

Notice that Figure 5-14 and Figure 5-15 both use a *merging* Inclusive Gateway to ensure that the correct number of Sequence Flow are joined together again. While there is no requirement that the *outgoing* flows of an Inclusive Gateway merge (they could each follow independent paths and never come back together), if the intention is to rejoin these threads together, then a *merging* Inclusive Gateway is needed. If a Parallel Gateway were used, then it would expect *incoming* Sequence Flow on all paths. If an Exclusive Gateway were used, it would not merge the paths together at all; instead each thread would pass straight through.

More details on each of the elements introduced are available in the BPMN Reference Section:

- Inclusive Gateways on page 148.
- Conditional Sequence Flow on page 170.

Exercise 4

After the Expense Report is received, a new account must be created if the employee does not already have one. The report is then reviewed for automatic approval. Amounts under $200 are automatically approved, whereas amounts equal to or over $200 require approval of the supervisor.

In case of rejection, the employee must receive a rejection notice by email. The reimbursement goes to the employee's direct deposit bank account. If the request is not completed in 7 days, then the employee must receive an "approval in progress" email

If the request is not finished within 30 days, then the process is stopped and the employee receives an email cancellation notice and must re-submit the expense report.

Exercise 5

After the Process starts, a Task is performed to locate and distribute any relevant existing designs, both electrical and physical. Next the design of the electrical and physical systems starts in parallel. Any existing or previous Electrical and Physical Designs are inputs to both Activities. Development of either design is interrupted by a successful update of the other design. If interrupted, then all current work is stopped and that design must restart.

In each department (Electrical Design and Physical Design), any existing designs are reviewed, resulting in an Update Plan for their respective designs (i.e. one in Electrical and another in Physical). Using the Update Plan and the existing Draft of the Electrical/Physical Design, a revised design is created. Once completed the revised design is tested. If the design fails the test, then it is sent back to the first Activity (in the department) to review and create a new Update Plan. If the design passes the test, then it tells the other department that they need to restart their work.

When both of the designs have been revised, they are combined and tested. If the combined design fails the test, then they are both sent back to the beginning to initiate another design cycle. If the designs pass the test, then they are deemed complete and are then sent to the manufacturing Process [a separate Process]. [18]

---

[18] Example answers to these Exercises will be made available online at http://www.bpmnreferenceguide.com/

Part II.   BPMN Reference Section

Chapter 6.   BPMN Reference Introduction

This Section provides a comprehensive stand-alone reference for BPMN modelers. Our assumption is that the reader will refer to this section from time to time; therefore, the reference section is organized conceptually, going through all aspects of behavior for a particular type of BPMN element in a logical fashion.

As we introduce each section, we have sought to highlight the aspects that will interest the Business Analyst and End-User (referred to as "Core"). These are differentiated from the more sophisticated aspects that will appeal to those who are looking to execute or simulate processes (referred to as "Advanced"). We also have sought to highlight the best practices that will help the modeler avoid incorrect or confusing models.

Remember that within this book, we have referred to the graphical elements of BPMN with Initial Capitals. Where an important concept is referenced (that is not a graphical BPMN element), we have used *italics* within the sentence.

Throughout this book, we use the concept of a *"token"* to explain some of the underlying behavior of a BPMN model. Think of *tokens* as moving along Sequence Flow and passing through the other objects of the Process. As a group, these other objects (Events, Activities, and Gateways) are called *flow objects*.

A *token* is a "theoretical" object that we use to create a descriptive "simulation" of the behavior (it is not currently a formal part of the BPMN specification). Using this mechanism, the performance of the Process (and its elements) is represented by describing how these theoretical *tokens* travel (or don't travel) down the available Sequence Flow paths and through the *flow objects*.

A *token* traverses Sequence Flow, from the start to the end (to the arrowhead), instantaneously (see Figure 6-1). That is, there is no time associated with the *token* travelling down a Sequence Flow.

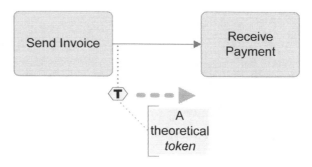

Figure 6-1—A *token* traveling down a Sequence Flow

As a *token* arrives at the *flow object*s, it may continue instantaneously or be delayed, depending on the nature of the *flow object*.
We will discuss how our theoretical *tokens* interact with each type
of *flow object*. The flow of a *token* between the *flow object*s, as they
operate normally, is known as *normal flow*. Occasionally, however,
an Activity will not operate normally. It might be interrupted by an
error or some other Event, and the resulting *token* flow is known
as *exception flow* (see section "Interrupting Activities with Events"
on page 99 for more detail on *exception flow*).

Chapter 7.   Activities

An Activity represents the work performed within a Business Process. It has a rounded-corner rectangle shape (see Figure 7-1 and Figure 7-2). An Activity will normally take some time to perform, will involve one or more resources from the organization, will usually require some type of *input*, and will usually produce some sort of *output*.

Activities are either *atomic* (i.e. they are the lowest level of detail presented in the diagram) or *compound* (i.e. they are non-*atomic* in the sense that you can drill down to see another level of process below). The *atomic* type of Activity is known as a Task and can be seen in Figure 7-1.

Figure 7-1—A Task

The *compound* type of Activity is called a Sub-Process (see Figure 7-2). The graphical difference between a Task and a Sub-Process is that a Sub-Process has a "plus sign" placed in the lower center of the shape, indicating that it can be opened up for more detail.

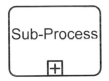

Figure 7-2—A Sub-Process

Depending on the process modeling tool, clicking or double clicking may expand the Sub-Process diagram in place or another window may open up. Double-clicking on a Task might also bring up more information such as the role assignment or other attributes of the Activity.[19]

Activities can be performed once, or they can have internally defined loops. An individual Task with a looping icon (see Figure 7-3) may define additional *conditions* for the Task to be performed

---

[19] BPMN uses attributes to store information about the Process (not shown graphically).

properly, e.g. an *output* being completed in a proper format. For more on Loop Activities see page 76.

Figure 7-3—A Task with an internal *loop*

Tasks

Use a Task when the detail of the Process is *not* broken down further; although that does not mean the behavior of the Task is not complex. Theoretically, a Task could always be broken down into a further level of detail. However, for the purposes of the model, no further detail is defined.

There are seven specialized types of Task:

- **None**—A generic or undefined Task, often used during the early stages of Process development.
- **Manual**—A non-automated Task that a human performer undertakes outside of the control of a workflow or BPM engine.
- **Receive**—Waits for a *message* to arrive from an external *participant* (relative to the Business Process). Once received, the Task is complete. These are similar in nature to the *catch* Message Event (see "Receiving Messages" on page 109).
- **Script**—Performs a modeler-defined script.
- **Send**—Dispatches a *message* to an external *participant*. These are similar in nature to the *throw* Message Event (see "Sending *Messages*" on page 108).
- **Service**—Links to some sort of service, which could be a Web service or an automated application.
- **User**—A typical "workflow" Task where a human performer carries out the Task with the assistance of a software application (usually scheduled through a List Manager or Inbox of some sort).

From the point of view of the Business Analyst, the only *core* Task type is the None Task type. All other Task types are for more advanced uses of BPMN.

Depending on the tool used, drilling down on a Task could reveal detailed information such as the role assignment or other attributes (presented in a dialog box).

Furthermore, different process-modeling tools may extend BPMN by adding graphical markers to the Task to help distinguish between different types of Tasks. Any markers added to a Task must not change the footprint of the Task (its overall shape) or conflict with any other standard BPMN element. This is a general rule for extending BPMN.

Best Practice: **Sending and Receiving Messages**—*The modeler could choose to use only Send and Receive Tasks, or to use only the throw and catch Message Intermediate Events. The Best Practice is to avoid mixing both approaches together in the same model.*

There are advantages and disadvantages to both approaches. Message Intermediate Events give the same result and have the advantage of being graphically distinguishable (whereas the Tasks are not). On the other hand, using Tasks, rather than the Events can enable the modeler to assign resources and simulate costs.

Sub-Processes

A Sub-Process represents a *compound* Activity. In this sense, "compound" means that its work is broken down into a finer level of detail (i.e. another Process). Thus, a "hierarchical" Process model is possible with different degrees of detail at each level.

There are two graphical representations of Sub-Processes:

- **Collapsed**—This version of the Sub-Process shape looks like a Task (a rectangle with rounded corners) with the addition of a small plus sign in the lower center (see Figure 7-4). The details of the Sub-Process are not visible in the diagram.

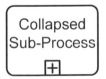

Figure 7-4—A *collapsed* Sub-Process (the detail hidden)

- **Expanded**—This version of the Sub-Process shape is "stretched" and opened such that the details of the Sub-Process are visible within the boundaries of the shape (see Figure 7-5). In this case, there is no marker in the lower center of the shape. However, some process modeling tools place a small minus sign in the lower center of the shape to indicate that the Sub-Process is collapsible. This is not part of standard BPMN, but is a valid extension.

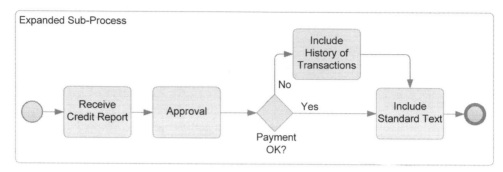

Figure 7-5—An *expanded* Sub-Process (the detail visible)

Types of Sub-Processes

There are two types of Sub-Processes:

- **Embedded**—A modeled Process that is actually part of the *parent* Process. *Embedded* Sub-Processes are not re-usable by other processes. All "process relevant data" used in the *parent* Process is directly accessible by the *embedded* Sub-Process (since it is part of the *parent*).
- **Reusable**—A separately modeled Process that could be used in multiple contexts (e.g., checking the credit of a customer). The "process relevant data" of the *parent* (calling) Process is not automatically available to the Sub-Process. Any data must be transferred specifically, sometimes reformatted, between the *parent* and Sub-Process. Note that the name of "Reusable" was changed from "Independent" in BPMN 1.1.

Depending on the tool or modeler preference, the Sub-Process diagrams may expand in place, or open up another diagram.

The distinction between embedded and *reusable* is not important for most modelers. However, as organizations develop a large number of process models, some of which they would want to re-use, the difference becomes more important—particularly when considering how data is used across the Process levels. These differences become even more important for organizations looking to use their process models in a BPM Suite, or within a Service Oriented Architecture.

Embedded Sub-Processes

An *embedded* Sub-Process is "part of" the Process. That is, it belongs only to the *parent* Process and is not available for any other

BPMN Modeling and Reference Guide

Process. In addition, the 'scope' of an *embedded* Sub-Process is 'local' to the *parent* Process in that it can use data that is stored with the *parent* Process without need for mapping or translation. For example, if data such as "Customer Name" or "Order Number" were part of the *parent* Process, then Activities within the *embedded* Sub-Process will have access to this data directly (without any special mapping between the elements).

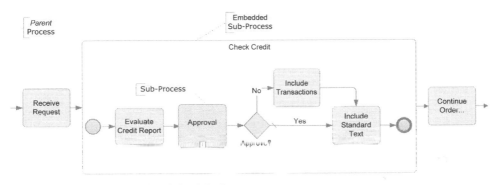

Figure 7-6—An *embedded* Sub-Process

An important characteristic of an *embedded* Sub-Process is that it can only begin with a None Start Event—i.e. without an explicit *trigger* such as a *message* (see Figure 7-6 above). Only *Top-Level* Processes can make use of *trigger*-based Start Events. The reason is that the *token* arriving from *parent* Process acts as the *trigger* for the Sub-Process.

Reusable Sub-Processes

As indicated by its name, a *reusable* Sub-Process may appear in multiple *parent* Processes—it is not "part of" the Process when it is instantiated. The *reusable* Sub-Process is a self-contained set of Activities. It provides a reference mechanism such that a single Process or service (in a Service Oriented Architecture) is available for any number of Processes that might invoke it.

These *reusable* Sub-Processes are "semi-independent" of the *parent* Process and can appear, unchanged, in multiple diagrams. For example, Figure 7-6 above, shows a "Check Credit" Sub-Process that could feature in many Processes where a customer's credit needs checking.

There is no graphical difference between *embedded* and *reusable* Sub-Processes. The difference is purely technical—tools will handle them in different ways. However, we expect that BPMN 2.0 will provide a graphical distinction between the two types of Sub-Processes.

Just like an *embedded* Sub-Process, a *reusable* Sub-Process must have a None Start Event. Likewise, the *token* from the *parent* Process is the *trigger* for the start of any Sub-Process.

Since a *reusable* Sub-Process typically provides a well-defined capability (e.g., checking credit), it might also act as a Top-Level Process in its own right. In which case, it can have a *trigger-laden* Start Event for this purpose (see Figure 7-7). Whenever a Process is initiated with a *trigger-based* Start Event (e.g., by a *message*), it will create a brand new context—i.e. a new *top-level* Process, not a Sub-Process. In these situations, the Sub-Process will have at least two Start Events (as a None Start Event is always required for usage as a Sub-Process).

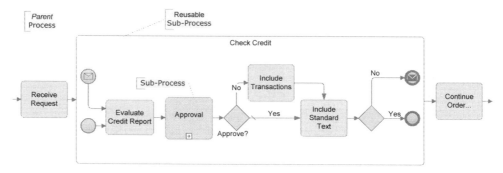

Figure 7-7—A *Reusable* Sub-Process can also be a *Top-Level* Process

Another characteristic of the *reusable* Sub-Process is that any data used by the Sub-Process is completely separate from the data of the invoking *parent* Process. The reuse capability relies on the fact that its data is completely self-contained. For example, if data such as "customer name" or "order number" is stored and used by the *parent* Process, and the *reusable* Sub-Process needs access to these data elements, it is not directly referenceable. Therefore, a mapping is required so that the *reusable* Sub-Process can have its own copies.

This is because *reusable* Sub-Processes exist independently of any particular *parent* Process, and therefore, the exact names of data elements may not exactly correspond. For example, a *parent* Process might name a data element "customer name," the *reusable* Sub-Process might have used a convention to shorten the name to "cust_name." Transferring data from the *parent* Process to the *reusable* Sub-Process will rely on a "mapping" between the data elements of the two levels. The mapping is required for both the *inputs* and the *outputs* of the *reusable* Sub-Process. The Activity *assignment* attribute handles the mapping of data, into and out of the Sub-Process (and as needed for any Activity).

This mapping is not a graphical aspect of BPMN, but it is important when dealing with execution or simulation environments. If the data elements have the exactly the same names, a process modeling tool might have facilities to do this mapping automatically. However, if the data elements have different names, then a modeler will have to choose the data elements that map together (perhaps supported by the modeling tool).

Connecting Activities

As described in more detail in the section on "Sequence Flow" on page 169, Sequence Flow connects *flow objects*, including Activities. Each Activity can have one or more *incoming* Sequence Flow and one or more *outgoing* Sequence Flow.

Typically, an Activity will tend to have a single *incoming* and a single *outgoing* Sequence Flow (see Figure 7-8).

Figure 7-8—Sequence Flow connects Tasks

Activity Behavior

As discussed earlier, the flow of the Process is determined by the paths of Sequence Flow. When a *token* arrives at an Activity, that Activity is then *ready* to start (see Figure 7-9). We will refer to the start and performance of an Activity as an *instance* of the Activity. A new *instance* is created whenever a *token* arrives at that Activity.

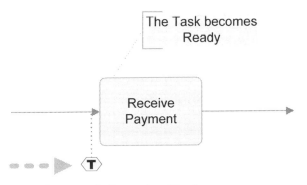

Figure 7-9—A *token* arriving at a Task

The Activity will remain *ready* (to perform) until all the defined requirements, such as *inputs* of data, become satisfied. Then the Activity is performed—i.e., it becomes "*active*" (see Figure 7-10).

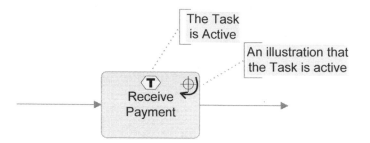

Figure 7-10—A *token* within an Active Task (the cross-hairs and curved arrow inside the Activity indicates that is now processing)

After the *instance* of the Activity is complete, the *token* then moves down the *outgoing* Sequence Flow, following the Process path (see Figure 7-11). For more on the life-cycle of an Activity see page 181.

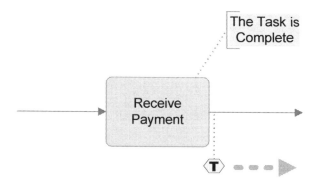

Figure 7-11—A *token* leaving a completed Task

With Multiple Incoming Sequence Flow

An Activity can have multiple *incoming* Sequence Flow. Each *incoming* Sequence Flow is independent from any other *incoming* Sequence Flow. This means that when a *token* arrives from one *incoming* Sequence Flow, the Activity is *ready* to start (see Figure 7-12). The Activity does not need to wait for *tokens* from any of the other *incoming* Sequence Flow.

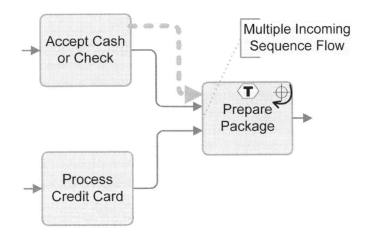

Figure 7-12—An example of a Task with multiple *incoming* Sequence Flow

If another *token* happens to arrive from any of the other *incoming* Sequence Flow (see Figure 7-13), then the Activity is now *ready* to start again. Separate *instances* of the Prepare Package Activity are performed for each *token* that arrives at the Activity. Technically, it is possible to have two or more *instances* of the Activity performed at the same time within the same Process.

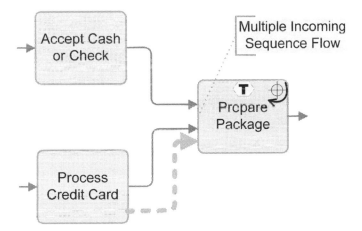

Figure 7-13—A second *incoming* Sequence Flow will generate another Prepare Package Activity *instance*

Note: Multiple *incoming* Sequence Flow for an Activity represents *uncontrolled* flow. To control the flow (i.e., have the Activity wait for other *incoming* Sequence Flow), then use a Parallel Gateway (see the section "Parallel Gateway Merging" on page 145 for more information).

With Multiple Outgoing Sequence Flow

An Activity can have multiple, *outgoing* Sequence Flow. Each *outgoing* Sequence Flow is independent from the other *outgoing* Sequence Flow. This means that when the Activity is complete a *token* moves off down <u>each</u> *outgoing* Sequence Flow (see Figure 7-14). This creates a set of parallel *tokens*. This mimics the behavior that would result from using a Parallel Gateway after the Activity (see the section entitled "Parallel Gateway Splitting" on page 144).

In order to select the *outgoing* Sequence Flow that will get the *token(s)*, use a Gateway to control the flow of the *tokens* (see the section "Gateways" on page 133 for more information). It is also possible to filter the output of *tokens* by placing *conditions* directly on the *outgoing* Sequence Flow (see the section Conditional Sequence Flow on page 170 for more information).

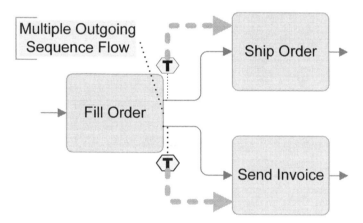

Figure 7-14—An Example of a Task with multiple *outgoing*
Sequence Flow

Looping

Looping represents another type of Activity behavior. There are three different ways to create loops in BPMN. Individual Activities can have looping characteristics as in Figure 7-15, or Sequence Flow can model the loop explicitly as in Figure 7-16.

Figure 7-15—An Activity with an internal loop

On an Activity, it is possible to define a loop *condition* that deter-mines the number of times to perform that Activity. There are two variations for Activity looping:

- **While Loop** (or While-Do)—shown by a looping symbol in the Activity. The loop *condition* is checked <u>before</u> the Activity is performed. If the loop *condition* turns out to be *true*, then the Activity is performed. If not, the Activity completes and the Process continues (a *token* moves down the *outgo-ing* Sequence Flow), even if the Activity was never per-formed. After the Activity is performed, then the Activity loops back to check the loop *condition* again. The cycle of checking the loop *condition* and performing the Activity continues until the loop *condition* is *False*.
- **Until Loop** (or Do While)—also shown by the same looping symbol in the Activity. The loop *condition* is tested <u>after</u> the Activity is performed. If the loop *condition* turns out to be *true*, then the Activity is performed again. If not, the Activ-ity completes and the Process continues (a *token* moves down the *outgoing* Sequence Flow). The cycle of checking the loop *condition* and performing the Activity continues until the loop *condition* is *false*.

Using Activity attributes, it is possible to set the maximum num-ber of loops (*loop maximum*) for both *while* and *until* loops. After the Activity has reached the *loop maximum*, it will stop (even if the loop *condition* is still *true*). The number of times that the Activity is performed is kept in a *loop counter* attribute that is automatically incremented for each loop. Some modeling tools do not currently support this sort of facility.

Figure 7-16 shows a visually obvious way to create loops using Sequence Flow to connect to an *upstream flow object*. Such a loop should include a Gateway or an infinite loop would occur. The Ga-teway checks the *conditions* on the *outgoing* Sequence Flow to de-termine whether to repeat the loop.

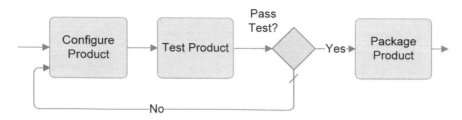

Figure 7-16—A loop with Sequence Flow

Multi Instance Activities

A subtly different mechanism is needed for behavior where an Activity should be performed many times with different data sets. For example, when a major corporation is checking financial results of all subsidiaries, it needs to carry this out many times.

Graphically represented with three vertical lines in the Activity, the Multi-Instance Activity (or ForEach) supports this behavior. The key point to understand here is that the Activity does not cycle around; each Activity Performance is distinct from the others (even though they are part of the same Process).

Figure 7-17—A Multi-Instance Activity

The value of the loop *condition* attribute determines the number of times that the Activity is performed. It is checked at the start of the Activity and then the Activity is "cloned" that number of times. The *condition* must resolve to an integer.

The individual *instances* of a Multi-Instance Activity might occur in *sequence* or in *parallel*. Attributes are available to control this behavior. Where this attribute is set to "Parallel," a further attribute is available to control how those *instances* merge back together again. The options (None, One, All or Complex) are equivalent to using Gateways to control parallel threads (paths) of a Process.

In BPMN 1.1, the Multi-Instance marker changed from two vertical lines to three vertical lines. The two vertical lines were often misinterpreted to mean a wait condition (it looked too much like a "pause" symbol on a tape or CD player).

Process Levels

In BPMN, it is possible to develop hierarchical structures for Processes through the use of one or more levels of Sub-Processes. In this book, we refer to a Process that contains a Sub-Process as the *parent* Process for the Sub-Process. Conversely, the Sub-Process is the *child* Process of the Process that contains it.

Of course, modelers might want to include a Sub-Process within another Sub-Process, creating as many Process levels as required. Each level is a complete Process. Figure 7-18 provides an example of a Sub-Process included within a *parent* Process.

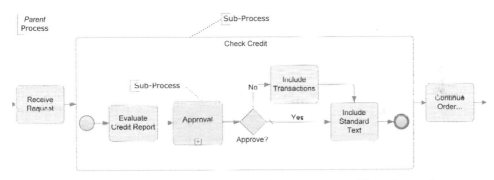

Figure 7-18—A Process with Sub-Processes: Showing three Process levels

The Process shown in Figure 7-18, above, has three Process levels—the Activity "Approval" in the "Check Credit" Sub-Process is itself a Sub-Process (*collapsed*).

Top-Level Processes

Any Process that does not have a *parent* Process is considered a *top-level* Process—i.e., a Process that is not a Sub-Process is a *top-level* Process (see Figure 7-19).

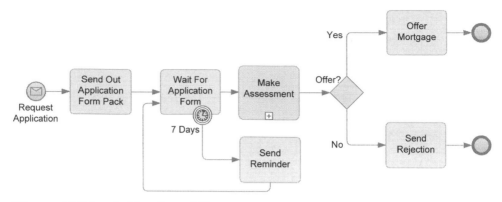

Figure 7-19—A *Top-Level* Process

The assumption is that a *top-level* Process is *triggered* by some external stimulus—i.e. outside the Process scope. This trigger is not always modeled and a None Start Event is used. In other cases, the Start Event will show the type of *trigger* used to initiate the Process. For example, a Message Start Event or a Timer Start Event (is in Figure 7-19, above).

Behavior Across Process Levels

To understand the way in which Process levels interact (across the levels) we again use *tokens*. When a *token* from the *parent* Process arrives at a Sub-Process (see Figure 7-20), it invokes the Start Event of that Sub-Process. However, note that the Sequence Flow of the *parent* Process does not extend into the Sub-Process. The Sequence Flow of the *parent* Process connects to the boundary of the Sub-Process and a different set of Sequence Flow and Activities (a different Process) is contained within the Sub-Process.

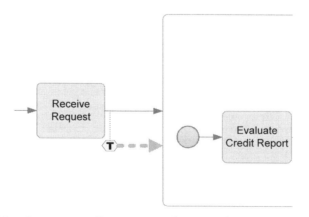

Figure 7-20—A *parent* Process *token* arrives at a Sub-Process (remainder of Sub-Process not visible)

The *token* from the *parent Process* now resides in the Sub-Process (see Figure 7-21). The presence of the *parent-level token* in the Sub-Process triggers the Start Event, thereby initiating the work of the Sub-Process (the Sub-Process is now *running*—as represented by the symbol next to the *token* in the figure). A *child* Process *token* is created by the Start Event and this *token* moves off down the *outgoing* Sequence Flow of the Start Event in the Sub-Process.

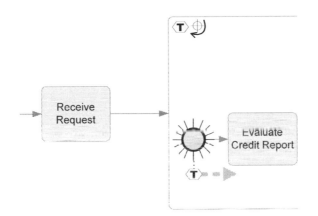

Figure 7-21—The Start Event of the Sub-Processes is triggered, creating a lower-level *token*

When the *child-level token* reaches the Sub-Process End Event, the End Event fires (see Figure 7-22). This signifies that the Sub-Process has completed its work (i.e., all the Sub-Process Activities have finished) and the *lower-level token* is consumed.

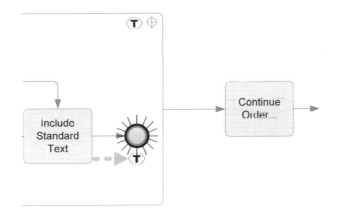

Figure 7-22—The Sub-Process *token* Arrives at the End Event

However, a Sub-Process is still *active* until all *threads* (paths) have completed. In an execution environment (BPM Suite), the system might track any outstanding work in a couple of ways—either by tracking *tokens* or the states of the Activities within the system.

Either way, when the Sub-Process finishes, the *parent-level token* moves down the *outgoing* Sequence Flow of the Sub-Process (see Figure 7-23), continuing the flow of the *parent* Process.

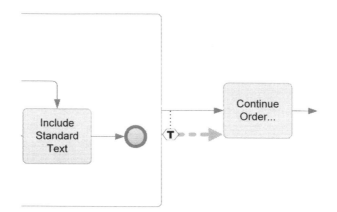

Figure 7-23—The *parent* Process continues after the Sub-Process completes

Remember that although Sequence Flow does not cross Process boundaries (Pools or Sub-Processes), Message Flow and Associations can cross these boundaries.

Connecting Sub-Processes

We have already discussed how Activities are connected (see "Connecting Activities" on page 73). Since Sub-Processes are a type of Activity, the same connection rules apply. However, there are more options when connecting an *expanded* Sub-Process than when connecting a Task.

So far, we have looked at the typical mechanism—connecting the Sequence Flow to the boundary of the Sub-Process (see Figure 7-24). The Start Event for the Sub-Process is inside the boundary and is not connected to the Sequence Flow of the *parent*-level Process.

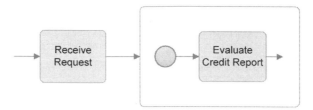

Figure 7-24—The Start Event is inside the Sub-Process

However, to provide greater clarity in Process interaction between levels, it is possible to place the Sub-Process Start Event <u>on its boundary</u> and then connect the *incoming* Sequence Flow directly to the required Start Event (see Figure 7-25). This capability is only a graphical convenience; otherwise a Start Event would not be placed on the boundary of the Sub-Process. Given this, the behavior of the two versions (Figure 7-24 and Figure 7-25) is exactly the same.

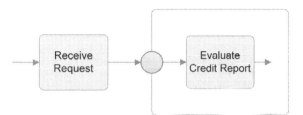

Figure 7-25—The Start Event on the Boundary

However, if the relationship between the *parent* Process and the Sub-Process is more complex, then the placement of the Start Events on the boundary of the Sub-Process can help clarify the flow between the *incoming* Sequence Flow (to the Sub-Process) and the Start Events of that Sub-Process.

In Figure 7-26, the path for one *incoming* Sequence Flow is intended for one of the Sub-Process's Start Events and the other *incoming* Sequence Flow is intended for the other Start Event.

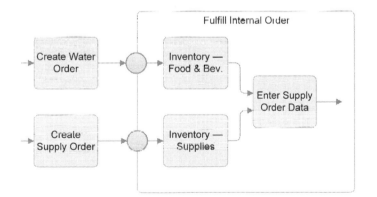

Figure 7-26—Multiple paths into a Sub-Process guided by Start Events on the boundary

This means that when a *token* arrives from the "Create Water Order" Task the <u>upper</u> Start Event of the Sub-Process will be triggered (see Figure 7-27).

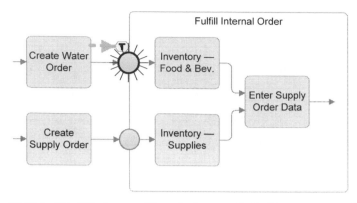

Figure 7-27—Multiple paths into a Sub-Process guided by Start Events on the boundary

However, when a *token* arrives from the "Create Supply Order" Task the <u>lower</u> Start Event of the Sub-Process will be triggered (see Figure 7-28).

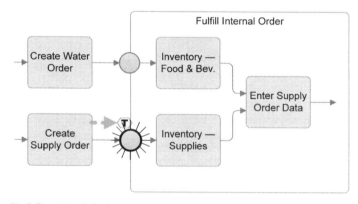

Figure 7-28—Multiple paths into a Sub-Process guided by Start Events on the boundary

Note that each time a Start Event triggers, a new *instance* of the Sub-Process is created. That is, if there is a "Water Order" and a "Supply Order," there will be separate *instances* of the Sub-Process for each order. Depending on the *upstream* structure of the Process (e.g. leveraging a Parallel Gateway), the two Sub-Process *instances* could operate in parallel, as part of a single *parent* Process *instance*. Alternatively, they could be a part of two separate *parent* Process *instances* (where an *upstream* Exclusive Gateway was used).

In BPMN 1.1, there were a few technical changes to enable a modeling tool to better support these logical connections (between the *parent* Process Sequence Flow and the Sub-Process Start Events).

Chapter 8.   Events

An Event is something that "happens" during the course of a Process. These Events affect the flow of the Process and usually have a *trigger* or a *result*. They can start, delay, interrupt, or end the flow of the Process.

Represented by circles, the style of the boundary (single line, double line, or thick line) indicates the type. The three types of Events are:

- Start Event (single thin line)
- Intermediate Event (double thin line)
- End Event (single thick line)

The next three sections explore these types of Events, introducing the various options available.

Start Events

A Start Event shows where a Process can begin. A Start Event is a small, open circle with a single, thin lined boundary (see Figure 8-1).

Figure 8-1—A Start Event

There are different types of Start Events to indicate the varying circumstances that can trigger the start of a Process. In fact these circumstances, such as the arrival of a *message* or a timer "going off," are called *triggers*. All BPMN Events were designed to have an open center such that markers for the different types of Event *triggers* could appear within the Event shape. A *trigger* is <u>not</u> required—such details can be hidden or added later.

There are six types of Start Events, each with its own graphical representation. The Events are divided into *core* and *advanced* types:

Core Start Events (see Figure 8-2):

- **None**—No *trigger* is defined.
- **Timer**—The *trigger* is specific date and time, or a regular date-time cycle (e.g., the first Friday of the month at 8am).

- **Message**—The *trigger* is a *message* arrives from another business entity or role (*participant*). For example, a client requests a review of their account.
- **Signal**—The *trigger* is a *signal* broadcast from another Process. For example, a Process broadcasts a change in the prevailing Interest Rate, triggering any number of other processes to start as a result.[20]

Core Start Events

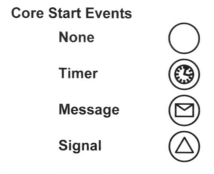

Figure 8-2—*Core* types of Start Events

Advanced **Start Events** (see Figure 8-3):

- **Conditional**—The *trigger* is a *condition expression* that must be satisfied for the Process to start.
- **Multiple**—Defines two or more triggers that can be any combination of *messages*, *timers*, *conditions*, or *signals* (any one of which will start the Process).

Advanced Start Events

Figure 8-3—*Advanced* types of Start Events

Modeling tools will also use different types of standard attributes to record the details of each type of Event (often not visible at the diagram level).

---

[20] We have included the use of *signals* in the *core* set of Events because of their usefulness. Understanding how to model using these features is considered essential for a Business Analyst to represent many of the desired behaviors.

Connecting Start Events

A key point to remember about a Start Event is that it can only have *outgoing* Sequence Flow. Sequence Flow is not allowed to connect *into* a Start Event (since a Start Event represents the start of the flow of a Process). Figure 8-4 shows an <u>incorrect</u> use of a Start Event (i.e., it has *incoming* Sequence Flow).

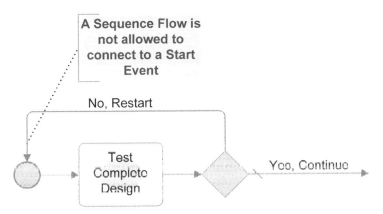

Figure 8-4—An <u>incorrect</u> use of a Start Event

The correct version of the Process fragment shown in Figure 8-4 would have the Sequence Flow connect back to the first Task (see Figure 8-5).

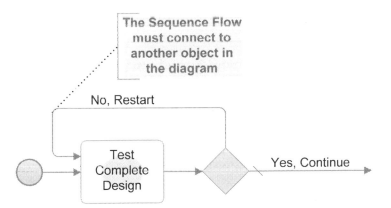

Figure 8-5—A <u>correct</u> version of Figure 8-4

In this case, in spite of the label of the Sequence Flow that loops backwards, the entire Process does not restart; it loops back to the first Activity.

The only way to restart a Process (at the Start Event) is to end the Process and then trigger the Start Event again. This would create a new *instance* of the Process.

Start Event Behavior

Start Events are where the flow of a Process starts, and, thus, are where *tokens* are created. When a Start Event is triggered, the *token* is generated (see Figure 8-6).[21]

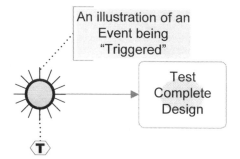

Figure 8-6—A *token* is generated when a Start Event is triggered

Immediately after the Start Event triggers and the *token* generated, the *token* will then exit the Start Event and travel down the *outgoing* Sequence Flow (see Figure 8-7).

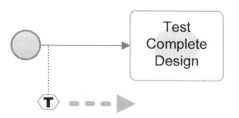

Figure 8-7—The *token* then exits the Start Event down the Sequence Flow

The None Start Event

A Start Event without a *trigger* is known as a None Start Event. It is used where the start of a Process is undefined. Since there is no *trigger* defined, there is no marker in the center of the shape (see Figure 8-8). Also, a None Start Event is <u>always</u> used to mark the start of Sub-Processes (dropping from one level to the next).

---

[21] The lines shown radiating out from the Start Event are for illustrative purposes and are not part of the BPMN specification.

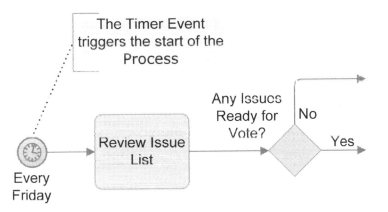

Figure 8-8—A None Start Event

Timer Start Events

Graphically, the Timer Start Event uses the clock marker within the Event shape (see Figure 8-9). It indicates that the Process is started (i.e., triggered) when a specific time condition has occurred. This could be a specific date and time (e.g., January 1, 2009 at 8am) or a recurring time (e.g., every Monday at 8am).

The Timer Event triggers the start of the Process

Any Issues Ready for Vote?

Review Issue List

No

Yes

Every Friday

Figure 8-9—A Timer Start Event used to Start a Process

Figure 8-9, above, provides an example of a Process, which is started every Friday, that reviews a set of issues that may be voted upon by a group.

Message Start Events

The Message Start Event represents a situation where a Process is initiated (i.e. triggered) by the receipt of a *message*. This type of Event has an envelope marker (see Figure 8-10).

A *message* is a direct communication between two business *participants*. These *participants* must be in separate Pools (i.e., they cannot be sent from another Lane inside a single Pool).

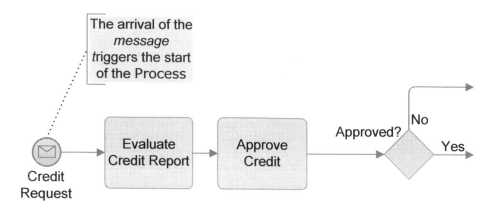

Figure 8-10—A Message Start Event used to Start a Process

Figure 8-10, above, provides an example where a "Credit Request" *message* triggers the start of a Process that will evaluate and approve (or not) the credit of the requester.

Signal Start Events

The Signal Start Event uses a triangle marker within the Event shape (see Figure 8-11). It indicates that the Process is started (i.e. triggered) when a *signal* is detected. This *signal* was broadcast communication from a business *participant* or another Process. *Signals* have no specific target or recipient—i.e. all Processes and *participants* can see the *signal* and it is up to each of them to decide whether or not to react. A *signal* is analogous to a flare or siren; anyone who sees the flare or hears the siren may, or may not, react.

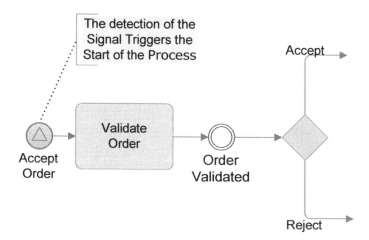

Figure 8-11—A Signal Start Event used to Start a Process

Unlike *messages, signals* can operate within a Process (perhaps between a Sub-Process and its *parent* calling Process), or across the Processes of different *participants*. Figure 8-11 above provides an example where an "Accept Order" *signal* triggers the start of a Process that will evaluate and accept (or not) the order for processing.

BPMN 1.1 added the Signal Start Event and removed the "Link Start Event". Signals provide a more general way of communicating between processes.

Conditional Start Events

The Conditional Start Event represents a situation where a Process is started (i.e., triggered) when a pre-defined *condition* becomes *true*. This type of Event has a lined paper marker (see Figure 8-12) This type of Event is usually triggered by some change in the "process relevant data" such as in a banking scenario, when the customers balance drops below a certain threshold. A *condition* is used to define the details of the change in data that is expected.

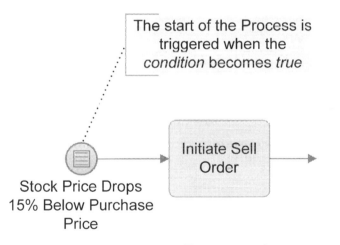

The start of the Process is triggered when the *condition* becomes *true*

Stock Price Drops
15% Below Purchase
Price

Initiate Sell
Order

Figure 8-12—A Conditional Start Event used to Start a Process

A *condition* is a natural language or computer language expression that tests some data. The test will result in an answer of *true* or *false*. The expected change occurs (i.e., the Event is triggered) when the result of the *condition* test is *true*. The *condition* for the Event must become *false* and then *true* again before the Event can be triggered again.

When creating a higher-level model (to document a Process), then a natural language *condition* is usually sufficient. For example, a *condition* for a Process that sells a stock:

"The Current Stock Price Drops 15 percent Below The Purchase Price"

While this kind of *condition* is sufficient at a documentation level, a model designed for execution (by a BPM engine) will require a more formal language that the system can understand.

For example, a formal definition of the same *condition* for the stock price might read:

"(dataObject[name="StockInfo"]/currentPrice) < ((dataObject[name="StockInfo"]/purchasePrice) * 0.85)

Figure 8-12, above, provides an example of a Process that is started by the above *condition* (the natural language version is displayed).

In BPMN 1.1, the Rule Start Event was renamed the Conditional Start Event as it represented a more accurate description of the behavior.

Multiple Start Events

The Multiple Start Event uses a pentagon marker within the Event shape (see Figure 8-13). It represents a collection of two or more Start Event *triggers*. The *triggers* can be any combination of *messages*, *timers*, *conditions*, and/or *signals*. Any one of those *triggers* will instantiate the Process—i.e., as soon as the *trigger* occurs, a new Process *instance* is generated and the flow will continue from that Start Event (ignoring other *instances* that may exist already). If one of the other *triggers* occurs, or the same *trigger* occurs again, then another Process *instance* is generated.

Figure 8-13—A Multiple Start Event

The icon for the Multiple Start Event has changed from a six-pointed star to a pentagon shape in BPMN 1.1 (as shown in Figure 8-3, above) .

Modeling with More than One Start Event

Most Processes have a single Start Event. However, it is possible to include more than one Start Event within a single Process (see

Figure 8-14). This is often needed where there are multiple ways that a Process can start, each starting at different point in the Process. Sometimes, as in the example below, the Start Events may lead to a different sequence of Activities, but this is not a requirement.

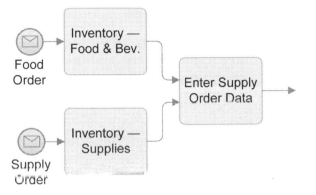

Figure 8-14—A Process with multiple Start Events

Each Start Event is independent of other Start Events in the Process. This means that the Process will start when <u>any one</u> of the Start Events within the Process is triggered. The Process will not wait for all the Start Events. If any other Start Event fires after the Process starts, then a separate *instance* (performance) of the Process is created.

Any Process, whether there is one Start Event or multiple, can have multiple *instances* of the Process active at the same time. Each time a Start Event (any Start Event) triggers, a new *instance* of the Process is created.

Start Events and Sub-Processes

Note that *trigger*-based Start Events can only feature in "Top-Level" Processes. *Trigger*-based Start Events are <u>never used</u> in Sub-Processes as it is the *parent* Process that invokes the start of the Sub-Process (when a *token* arrives from the *parent* Process to the Sub-Process).

Start Events Are Optional

Most Processes have a Start Event to show the position of the start of the Process or to indicate the *trigger* that will start the Process. However, a Process, either a *top-level* Process or a Sub-Process, is not <u>required</u> to have a Start Event (see Figure 8-15).

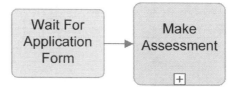

Figure 8-15—The Start of a Process _Without_ a Start Event

If the Start Event is element not used, then the first *flow object* that does not have an *incoming* Sequence Flow represents the position where the Process starts. This representation will behave as if an invisible Start Event existed, connected to the first element in the Process (see Figure 8-16). If there are multiple elements that do not have *incoming* Sequence Flow, then all of those elements will be initiated at the start of the Process.

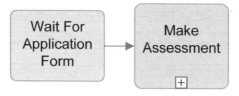

Figure 8-16—The Process Acts as if there is a Virtual Start Event

The use of the Start Event is tied to the use of an End Event in the Process. If a Start Event is not used, then an End Event is not used either. If an End Event is used, then a Start Event must also be used.

Best Practice: **Use of Start Events**—*In general, we recommend that modelers use Start and End Events.*

However, there are situations where it is more fitting to create a Process without them. Usually, a modeler will do this for small and simple Sub-Processes, when the start and end of the flow is clearly understood. One example of this is the concept of a "parallel box"—a Sub-Process with a set of Activities that must run in parallel (see Figure 8-17). By modeling this behavior with a Sub-Process without Start and End Events, the resulting diagram is more compact and less cluttered.

BPMN Modeling and Reference Guide

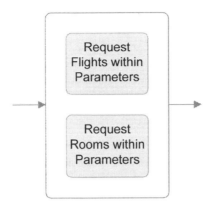

Figure 8-17—An Example of a "Parallel Box" where Start and End Events <u>are not</u> used

Figure 8-18 shows the alternative method of modeling this same behavior. While this method will deliver the appropriate behavior, visually, it is less appealing.

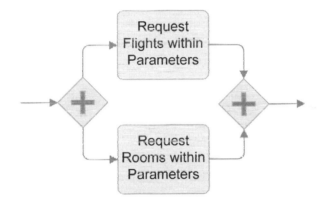

Figure 8-18—An alternative method of a modeling the "Parallel Box" behavior

To provide the capability to model such things as "parallel boxes" (as seen as Figure 8-17, above), Start and End Events were made optional in BPMN.

Intermediate Events

An Intermediate Event indicates where something happens/occurs after a Process has started and before it has ended. An Intermediate Event is a small, open circle with a double, thin lined boundary (see Figure 8-19).

◯

Figure 8-19—An Intermediate Event

Intermediate Events are placed within the Process flow to represent things that happen during the normal operations of the Process and usually occur in between Activities. They may also interrupt the normal processing of an Activity.

There are nine different types of Intermediate Events, each with its own graphical representation (see Figure 8-21). Each type of Intermediate Events can either *throw* or *catch* the event.

Again, we have divided them into *core* and *advanced* types:

Core Intermediate Events (see Figure 8-20):

- **None**—No *trigger* is defined.
- **Timer**—The *trigger* is based on a specific date and time, or a regular date-time cycle (e.g., the first Friday of the month at 8am).
- **Message**—The *trigger* is a *message*. The *message* must be sent to, or received from, another business entity in the Process. These business entities (*participants*), if shown in the diagram, are represented by Pools.
- **Signal**—The *trigger* is a *signal* that is broadcast or received.

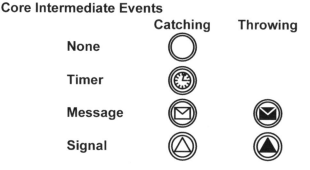

Figure 8-20—Core types of Intermediate Events (both *throw* and *catch*)

Advanced Intermediate Events (see Figure 8-21):

- **Error**—Defines an Event that will usually disrupt the Process or require correction (see Interrupting Activities with Events on page 99).

- **Cancel**—Used to cancel a Transaction Sub-Process (see "Compensation and Transactions" on page 183).
- **Compensation**—Used to establish the behavior required to "undo" Activities in case a Transaction Sub-Process is cancelled or needs to be rolled-back (see "Compensation and Transactions" on page 183).
- **Conditional**—Defines a rule that must be satisfied in order for the Process to continue.
- **Link**—Used to create a visual "Go To" mechanism, hiding long Sequence Flow or to establish off-page connectors for printing.
- **Multiple**—Defines two or more triggers that can be any combination of *messages, timers, errors, conditions*, or *signals*.

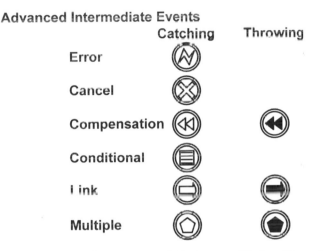

Figure 8-21—**Advanced types of Intermediate Events (both *throw* and *catch*)**

This <u>graphical</u> difference between *catch* and *throw* is new in BPMN 1.1. Other Intermediate Event related changes for BPMN 1.1 include the addition of the Signal Intermediate Event, the change of the marker for the Multiple Intermediate Event, and the renaming of the Rule Intermediate Event to the Conditional Intermediate Event.

Intermediate Event Behavior

When a *token* arrives from an *incoming* Sequence Flow to an Intermediate Event, it will do one of two things:

- It waits for something to happen (i.e., wait for the circumstance defined on the *trigger*—see "Receiving Messages on page 109 for an example). This type of Event is known as a *catching* Intermediate Event. The internal markers for all *catching* Intermediate Events have a white infill. This includes Start Events, since these types of Events also wait to be triggered.
- It immediately fires (effectively creating the circumstance defined on the *trigger*—see "Sending *Messages* on page 108 for an example). This type of Event is known as a *throwing* Intermediate Event. The internal markers for all *throwing* Intermediate Events have a black infill. This includes End Events, as they also immediately trigger.

The Events that can _catch_ are:

- Message
- Timer
- Error
- Cancel
- Compensation
- Conditional
- Link
- Signal
- Multiple (catches any incoming event in the list)

A *token* arriving at a *catch* Intermediate Event would wait until the *trigger* occurs. Then the *token* would leave immediately and move down the *outgoing* Sequence Flow.

Events that can _throw_ are:

- Message
- Compensation
- Link
- Signal
- Multiple (throws all events in the list)

A *token* arriving at a *throw* Intermediate Event would immediately fire the *trigger*. It would then leave immediately and travel down the *outgoing* Sequence Flow.

BPMN Modeling and Reference Guide

Connecting Intermediate Events

Intermediate Events are either placed within the *normal flow* of a Process (i.e. between Activities), or they are attached to the boundary of an Activity to trigger an <u>interruption</u> of that Activity—this is discussed in more detail later—see "Interrupting Activities with Events."

Since Intermediate Events are not Gateways (discussed further in "Gateways" on page 133), they are not used to split or merge Sequence Flow. Thus, only <u>one</u> *incoming* and only <u>one</u> *outgoing* Sequence Flow is allowed for an Intermediate Event within *normal flow* (see Figure 8-22).

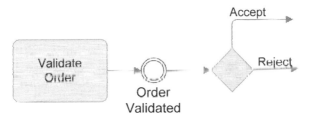

Figure 8-22—An Intermediate Event within the *normal flow*

Interrupting Activities with Events

BPMN uses Events attached to the boundary of an Activity as a way of modeling *exceptions* to the normal flow of the Process. The attached Event indicates that the Activity should be interrupted when the Event is triggered (see Figure 8-23). These types of Events always *catch* the relevant *trigger,* thus the *trigger* marker will always be white-filled (see Figure 8-19, above).

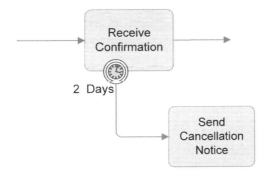

Figure 8-23—An Intermediate Event attached to the boundary of an Activity

The way that BPMN handles *exceptions* is an innovation for process modeling notations. The normal way of exiting an Activity is

for the work in the Activity to complete and for the *outgoing* connector (a Sequence Flow) to show the path to the next Activity (or
other *flow object*). As a means of accentuating the *exception* paths
within a Process, the BPMN approach of attaching Intermediate
Events to the boundary of an Activity provides a natural and obvious way to show the non-normal ways of exiting an Activity. Both
Tasks and Sub-Processes are interrupted in the same way.

The types of Events that can interrupt an Activity are:

- Timer
- Message
- Error
- Cancel
- Conditional
- Signal
- Multiple

A Compensation Intermediate Event can also be attached to the
boundary of an Activity. However, these Events do not interrupt
the Activity since they are only operational <u>after</u> an Activity has
completed. See "Compensation and Transactions" on page 183 for
more details about Compensation Events.

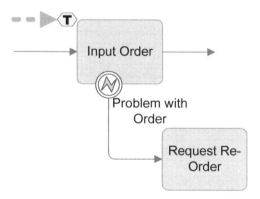

**Figure 8-24—A *token* arrives at a Task with an attached Error
Intermediate Event**

Tracing a *token* allows us to show how *exception handling* works.
The *token* leaves the previous *flow object* and arrives at the Activity with the attached Intermediate Event. (see Figure 8-24 above).
[22]

---

[22] We use an Error Intermediate Event to demonstrate the behavior, but any of the
interrupting Intermediate Events listed above could have been used.

The *token* enters the Activity and starts the work and life-cycle of the Activity (for more on this issue, see section "The Life-Cycle of an Activity" on page 181). At the same time, another *token* is created and resides in the Intermediate Event on its boundary (see Figure 8-25). This readies the interrupting Intermediate Event to fire. If the attached Event happens to be a *timer*, then the clock is started.

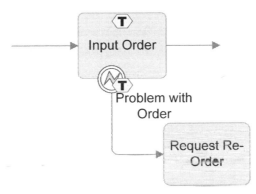

Figure 8-25—A *token* Resides in Both the Task and the Error Intermediate Event

The Activity and attached Intermediate Event become involved in a *race condition*. Whichever one finishes first will win the *race* and take control of the Process with its *token*. If the Activity finishes before the *trigger* occurs (in this case *error*), then the *token* from the Activity moves down the normal *outgoing* Sequence Flow of the Activity (see Figure 8-26) and the additional *token* is consumed.

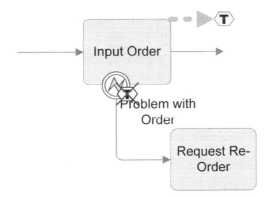

Figure 8-26—The *token* leaves the Task before the Error Intermediate Event fires

However, if the attached Intermediate Event triggers before the Activity finishes, then the Activity is interrupted (all work stops). In this case, the *token* from the Event moves down its *outgoing*

Sequence Flow, but not the normal *outgoing* Sequence Flow of the Activity (see Figure 8-27). The *token* that was on the Activity is consumed.

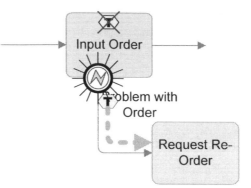

Figure 8-27—The Error Intermediate Event is *triggered* interrupting the Task

The flow from the Intermediate Events can go anywhere. It can go down a completely new path, it can rejoin the normal path, or it can loop back *upstream*.

The Events that can interrupt can attach to either Tasks or Sub-Processes. The exception to this is the Cancel Intermediate Event, which is only used on Transaction Sub-Processes (see "Compensation and Transactions" on page 183).

None Intermediate Events

As with a Start Event, a *trigger* is not always required for an Intermediate Event. An Intermediate Event without a *trigger* is known as a None Intermediate Event (as in Figure 8-19, above).

None Intermediate Events are mainly used to document that certain Activities have completed or that the Process has reached a defined state, such as a milestone. The name of the Event can often provide enough information for these purposes.

For a None Intermediate Event, no circumstance is defined (i.e. there is no *trigger*). Therefore, it fires immediately (see Figure 8-28).

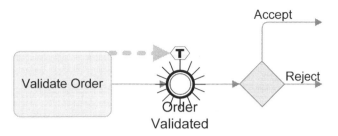

Figure 8-28—A *token* Arrives at an Intermediate Event

Immediately after triggering, the *token* moves down the *outgoing* Sequence Flow, continuing the Process (see Figure 8-29).

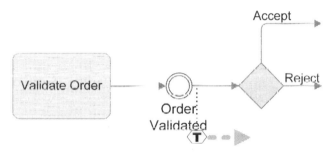

Figure 8-29—A *token* Leaves an None Intermediate Event

Timer Intermediate Events

The *Timer* Intermediate Event uses the clock marker within the Event shape (see Figure 8-30, below). Timer Intermediate Events can only *catch*. They add time-based dependencies within a Process and are either inserted into the Sequence Flow to create a delay, or attached to the boundary of an Activity to create a deadline or "time-out" condition. Timer Intermediate Events can also be used as part of an Event-Based Gateway (see page 140).

When a *token* arrives at a Timer Intermediate Event, the "clock starts" and the *token* waits for the specified time-related condition to occur (see Figure 8-30).

Figure 8-30—A *token* leaving a *Timer* Intermediate Event

Delays

When inserted between Activities in a Process, the Timer Intermediate Event represents a *delay* in the flow of a Process. Timer Intermediate Events can represent a specific date and time (e.g., wait until April 15, at 5pm), a relative time (e.g., wait 6 days), or a relative repetitive date (e.g., wait until next Monday at 8am).

Figure 8-31—A Timer Intermediate Event creating a *delay* in the Process

When the timer "goes off"—i.e. the specified time condition occurs—in this case, 6 days after the timer started, then the *token* moves down the Event's *outgoing* Sequence Flow (see Figure 8-30) and the Process continues.

To show how a delay *Timer* behaves, we trace a *token* through the example for the above figure. The *token* leaves the previous *flow object* and arrives at the Timer Intermediate Event (see Figure 8-32). The *flow object* that precedes the Timer can be an Activity, Gateway, or another Intermediate Event.

Figure 8-32—A *token* arrives at a Timer Intermediate Event

The *token* will remain at the Timer Intermediate Event (see Figure 8-33) until the clock reaches the time setting of the Event (i.e., the "alarm goes off").

The clock for relative time *delays* (e.g., 6 days) starts when the *token* arrives at the Event. The clock for specific and recurring time/dates is always compared with an actual (or simulated) calendar.

Note that if a specific date and time is set (e.g., January 1, 2007 at 8am) and that date and time has already occurred <u>before</u> the Timer Intermediate Event is active (i.e., before the *token* arrives), then the Event will never occur. Relative time and date settings cannot fail as the clock starts only when the Event triggers.

Best Practice: **Setting Timers**—*avoid specific date and time conditions as they inhibit the re-usability of the process.*

Figure 8-33—The *token* **will be** *delayed* **until the Timer is triggered**

When the Event is finally triggered, the *token* immediately exits the Event and moves off down the *outgoing* Sequence Flow (see Figure 8-34).

Figure 8-34—When the Timer is triggered, the *token* **continues**

Deadlines and Time-Outs

As discussed above, Timer Intermediate Events can also interrupt an Activity. When the Activity starts, so does the *timer*. If the Activity finishes first, then it completes normally and the Process continues normally. If the *timer* goes off before the Activity is completed, the Activity is immediately interrupted and the Process continues down the Sequence Flow from the Timer Intermediate Event (see Figure 8-35).

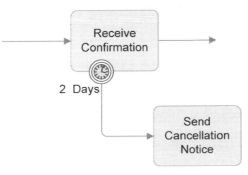

Figure 8-35—An Activity with a *time-out*

The behavior of the attached Timer Intermediate Events, and other interrupting Events, is described in "Interrupting Activities with Events on page 99.

Non-Interrupting Time-Outs

As we described in the above section, an attached Timer Intermediate Event interrupts an Activity when triggered. However, there are times when a *timer* might need to *trigger* additional Activities, <u>without</u> interrupting the Activity. For example, if the work of an Activity has not finished in the expected time, then the desired behavior is often required to trigger an email to the Performer's manager to expedite the situation. We refer to this type of scenario as a Non-Interrupting Event behavior.

In BPMN 1.1, it is impossible to use an attached Intermediate Event to create Non-Interrupting Event behavior. However, there are "Process Patterns" that easily resolve this requirement.

Figure 8-36 provides an example of a Process Pattern that solves this problem. The pattern relies on a Sub-Process with the Timer Intermediate Event set up in a parallel flow to the Activity, which ends with a Terminate End Event. Both the Activity and the Timer Intermediate Event follow a Start Event.

The *timer* starts at the same time as the Activity. If the *timer* triggers before the completion of the "Receive Confirmation" Activity, then a reminder is sent without interrupting the Activity. The *timer* is placed in a *loop* so that reminders are sent out every two days. When the Activity eventually finishes, the work moves to a Terminate End Event, which will stop all the Activity of the Sub-Process, including the *Timer* loop. The flow then continues at the level of *parent* Process. See also Terminate End Event on page 128.

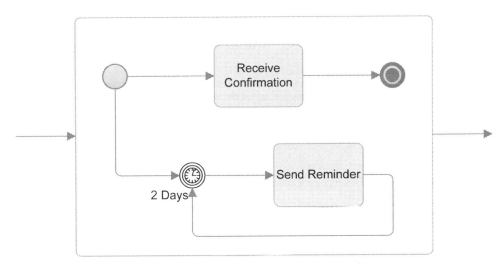

Figure 8-36—A Delay Timer Intermediate Event Used for Escalation

Process Pattern: The example shown in Figure 8-36, above, is an example of a "Process Pattern." This pattern can be used with different catch Intermediate Events (replacing the Time Intermediate Event) to create various non-interrupting behaviors based on messages, signals, or other types of triggers.

Another set of examples is provided in the opening scenario introduction in the section on "Setting Timers" on page 40, and also in "Another Approach to Escalation" on page 57.

In the next version of BPMN (BPMN 2.0), a *non-interrupting* capability is being built into Intermediate Events that are attached to an Activity boundary. This will enable the use of attached Events to either *interrupt* an Activity, or to *trigger* a Non-Interrupting Event. Process patterns like Figure 8-36 will still be valid, but no longer necessary. The notation for Non-Interrupting Events is not yet finalized, so we cannot provide an example.

Message Intermediate Events

The Message Intermediate Event is distinguished from other types of Intermediate Events by the envelope marker placed within the Event shape (see Figure 8-37). *Messages* are different from *signals* in that they are directed between Process *participants*—i.e. they <u>always</u> operate <u>across</u> Pools. They <u>cannot</u> be used to communicate between Lanes within a Pool.

"Catching"   "Throwing"

Figure 8-37—Message Intermediate Events

As shown in the figure above, there are two types of Message Intermediate Events: *throwing* and *catching*—i.e. sending and receiving.[23]

Sending *Messages*

One type of Message Intermediate Event is a *throwing* Event that sends a *message*. Its internal marker is a black-filled envelope (see Figure 8-21, above). This type of Event indicates that the Process will send a *message* at that point in the Process.

When a *token* arrives at a *throwing* Message Intermediate Event, it immediately triggers the Event, which sends the *message* to a specific *participant* (see Figure 8-38).

Figure 8-38—A *token* arriving at a *throwing* Message Intermediate Event

Immediately after the *message* is sent, the *token* moves down the *outgoing* Sequence Flow (see Figure 8-39), continuing the Process.

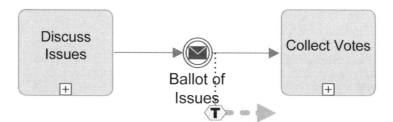

Figure 8-39—The *token* leaves a Message Intermediate Event

---

[23] In the examples provided here, we show Message Intermediate Events within the *normal flow* of the Process. We have not shown the Message Flow emanating from these Events that connect to an external *participant*. For more on Message Flow see page 173.

Receiving Messages

The other type of Message Intermediate Event *catches*—i.e., it waits for a *message* to arrive. The internal marker is a white-filled envelope (see Figure 8-21, above).

When a *token* arrives at a *catching* Message Intermediate Event in *normal flow*, the Process pauses until the *message* arrives (see Figure 8-40). Note that if a BPM Suite is executing the model, and the *message* arrives before the Message Intermediate Event is "active" (i.e., before the *token* arrives), then the *message* is ignored. In such a situation, the Message Intermediate Event will wait indefinitely unless the *message* is sent again.

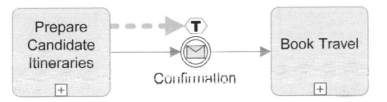

Figure 8-40—A *token* arriving at a *catching* Message Intermediate Event

If the *token* is waiting at the Intermediate Event and the *message* arrives, then the Event triggers. The *token* immediately moves down the *outgoing* Sequence Flow, continuing the Process (see Figure 8-41).

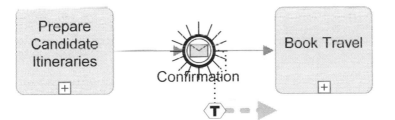

Figure 8-41—A *token* leaving a *catching* Message Intermediate Event

Message Intermediate Events might also appear attached to the boundary of an Activity as a *catch*. If the Event occurs, then the Activity is interrupted and the *token* leaves via the Sequence Flow attached to the Message Intermediate Event. For more on the precise nature of this, see the "Deadlines and Time-Outs" section on page 105.

Message Intermediate Events can also form part of an Event-Based Gateway (see page 140).

Signal Intermediate Event

Like Signal Start Events, the Signal Intermediate Event uses the triangle marker within the Event shape (see Figure 8-42). As with the Message Intermediate Event, there are two types of Signal Intermediate Events—*throwing* and *catching*.

Figure 8-42—Signal Intermediate Events

Examples of how Signal Events are used can be found in the section "Using Signal Events" on page 112.

Signal Events are a new feature of BPMN 1.1. They replace some of the functionality of Link Events, add new capabilities and enable a wide range of process patterns.

Broadcasting a Signal

The *throw* Signal Intermediate Event broadcasts. When a *token* arrives, it immediately triggers the Event, which broadcasts the *signal* to whatever other Events might be waiting for it (see Figure 8-43); it does not know anything about Events that might wait to catch the Signal. Its internal marker is a black-filled triangle.

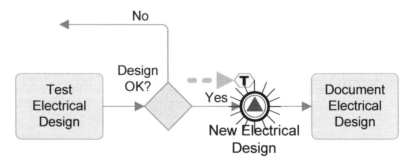

Figure 8-43—A *token* arriving at a *throwing* Signal Intermediate Event

Immediately after the *signal* is broadcast the *token* is sent down the *outgoing* Sequence Flow (see Figure 8-44), continuing the Process.

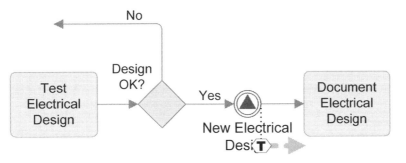

Figure 8-44—A _token_ leaving a _throwing_ Signal Intermediate Event

Receiving A Signal

The _catching_ Signal Intermediate Event waits for a _signal_ to arrive; the Process pauses until the _signal_ is detected. Its internal marker is a white-filled triangle.

When a _token_ arrives at a Signal Intermediate Event, the Process waits to detect the _signal_ (see Figure 8-45). Note that if the _signal_ arrives <u>before</u> the Signal Intermediate Event is ready—i.e. before the _token_ arrives, then the _signal_ is ignored. Unless the same _signal_ is sent again, the Process will wait indefinitely.

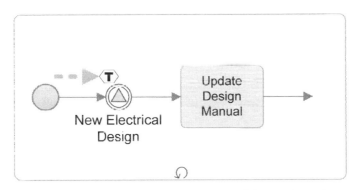

Figure 8-45—A _token_ arriving at a _catching_ Signal Intermediate Event

When the Signal Intermediate Event is identified (i.e. the Event fires), then the _token_ moves down the _outgoing_ Sequence Flow, and the Process continues (see Figure 8-46).

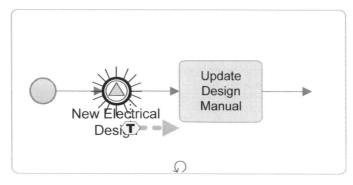

Figure 8-46—A *token* leaving a *catching* Signal Intermediate Event

Using Signal Events

Signal Events provide a general communication capability within and between Processes. They have some similarities to Message Events. Like Message Events, Signal Events have two types: one type sends or *throws* the *signal* and the other type receives or *catches* the *signal*. Unlike Link Events, Signal Events do not have to be used in pairs. A given Process can have just one *throw* or *catch* Signal Event.

On the one hand, a *message* is directed towards a specific target (i.e., another *participant* in a business-to-business relationship), whereas *signals* are broadcast generally. Think of *signals* as being like a signal flare. They fire and any number people looking might choose to react (or not). However, *signals* also have a name—therefore, *catching* Events can filter out *signals* that do not have the correct name (or they can be set to react to any *signal*).

There are several ways to use Signal Events including:

- Exception handling.
- Chaining Processes together; that is, signaling the start of one Process after the completion of another.
- Highlighting that a specific *milestone* has occurred.
- Inter-Process communication—especially useful where parallel paths of activity require coordination.
- As part of an Event-Based Gateway (see page 140).

Signal Events can operate across Process levels (across Sub-Process to *parent*, vice versa, or between Sub-Processes) or even across Pools. For example, a Signal Event could trigger status reports to a customer, indicating that the Process had reached an agreed milestone (the customer and the organization are *participants* operating within their own Pools).

Figure 8-47 presents a *milestone* example in which there are two Sub-Processes. The two Sub-Processes send *signals* back to the *parent* Process. The first Sub-Process also sends a *signal* to the second Sub-Process. The Sub-Processes are designed for re-use (in other Processes). Thus, to work well with each other and their *parent* Process, they must send *signals* at the appropriate times.

The "Develop Book Cover" Activity in the middle Sub-Process must wait until the "Develop Book Text & Main Concepts" Activity in the upper Sub-Process has completed. Since Sequence Flow cannot cross Sub-Process boundaries, Signal Events handle the communication and synchronize the two Sub-Processes.

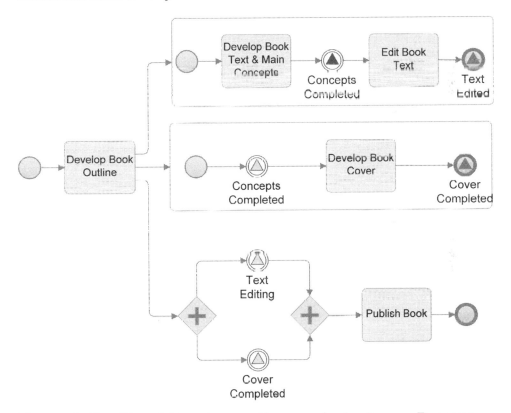

Figure 8-47—Signal Events can Communicate Across Process levels

In addition to the above *milestone* constraint, the "Publish Book" Activity in the *parent* Process must wait until the "Edit Book Text" Activity in the upper Sub-Process <u>and</u> the "Develop Book Cover" Activity in the middle Sub-Process have completed. To do this, the *parent* Process detects the *signal* from each of the Sub-Processes.

Tracing a *token* through the above example, we start at the point where both of the Sub-Processes have begun their work (see Figure 8-48). Each Start Event will generate a *token* and send them down the Sequence Flow. The *token* in the upper Sub-Process will go to the "Develop Book Text & Main Concepts" Activity. The *token* in the lower Sub-Process will go to the *catch* Signal Event, which will cause the Event to wait for a *signal*.[24]

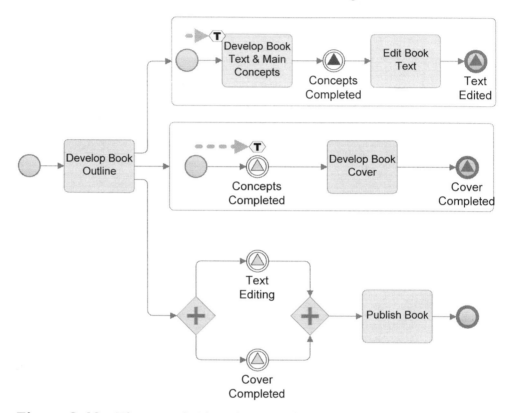

Figure 8-48—The *catch* Signal Event in the lower Sub-Process waits for a *signal*

Eventually the "Develop Book Text & Main Concepts" Activity in the upper Sub-Process will finish and send the *token* to the *throw* Signal Event (see Figure 8-49).

---

[24] *Tokens* are also sent to the *catching* Signal Intermediate Events in the *parent* Process, but we will not trace them for this example.

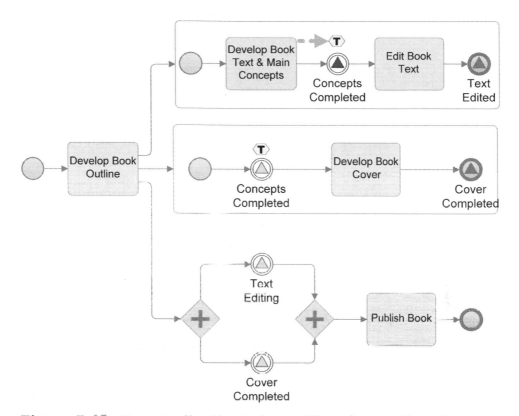

Figure 8-49—Eventually the *token* will arrive at the *throw* Signal Event in the upper Sub-Process

When the *token* arrives at the *throw* Signal Event in the upper Sub-Process it triggers the Event that causes the broadcast of the *signal* (see Figure 8-50). After the *signal* fires, the *token* continues down the *outgoing* Sequence Flow to the "Edit Book Text" Task.

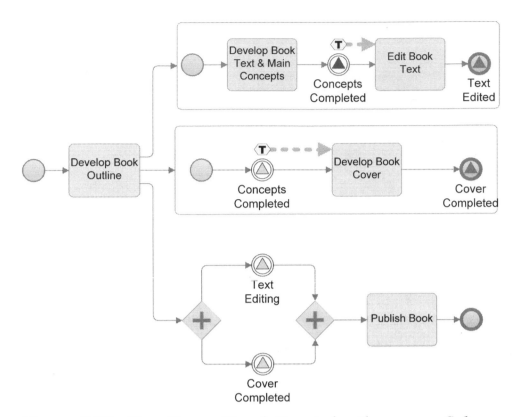

Figure 8-50—The *throw* Signal Event in the upper Sub-Process fires, which is detected by the *catch* Signal Event in the lower Sub-Process

In the lower Sub-Process, the *catch* Signal Event detects the *signal* broadcast by the upper Sub-Process. This will trigger the Event, which means that the *token* moves off to the "Develop Book Cover" Activity so that it can begin its work.[25]

Error Intermediate Events

The Error Intermediate Event is used to handle the occurrence of an *error* that would necessitate the interrupting of an Activity (to which it is attached). An *error* is generated when there is a critical problem in the processing of an Activity. *Errors* can be generated by applications or systems involved in the work (which are trans-

[25] Note that the BPMN specification does not define the precise mechanism used to support *signals*—i.e., the specification is implementation independent. At its simplest level, people might interpret the signals sent between each other, or a sophisticated software infrastructure such as Message Queuing might ensure that a BPM Engine (workflow engine) detected the relevant changes in state.

parent to the Process) or by End Events (see page 129). The Error Intermediate Event uses a lightning bolt marker within the Event shape (see Figure 8-51).

Figure 8-51—An Error Intermediate Event

This Event can only be used when attached to the boundary of an Activity, thus it can only be used to *catch* an *error*, never to *throw* an *error*. The Error End Event is used to *throw* an *error* (see "Error End Event" on page 129). When an *error* occurs all work will stop for that Process; thus it does not make sense to use an Intermediate Event to *throw* an *error*, since no further work takes place.

When this Event is triggered, then all work within the Activity is stopped. The Activity can be a Task or a Sub-Process. See "Interrupting Activities with Events on page 99 for an example of the behavior of this Event.

Cancel Intermediate Event

The Cancel Intermediate Event is designed to handle a situation where a *transaction* is *canceled*.[26] The Cancel Intermediate Event uses a white filled "X" marker within the Event shape (see Figure 8-52).

Figure 8-52—A Cancel Intermediate Event

Cancel Intermediate Events can only *catch* a *transaction cancellation*; they are not able to *throw* them. The Cancel End Event throws the cancellation (see "Cancel End Event" on page 130).

Furthermore, the Cancel Intermediate Event can only be attached to the boundary of a Transaction Sub-Process. It can be triggered by a Cancel End Event within the Sub-Process, or through a cancellation received through the *transaction protocol* assigned to the Transaction Sub-Process. When triggered, the Transaction Sub-Process is interrupted (all work stops) and the Sub-Process is *rolled-back*, which may result in the *compensation* of some of the

[26] A *transaction* is represented by a Transaction Sub-Process.

Activities within the Sub-Process. See "Compensation and Trans-actions" on page 183 for more details on how Transaction Sub-Processes are cancelled.

Compensation Intermediate Event

The Compensation Intermediate Event is distinguished from other types of Intermediate Events by the "rewind" symbol marker that is placed within the Event shape (see Figure 8-53).

Catching   **Throwing**

Figure 8-53—Compensation Intermediate Events

As shown in the figure above, there are two types of Compensa-tion Intermediate Events: *throwing* and *catching*—i.e. sending and receiving. The *catching* Compensation Intermediate Event can only be used by attaching them to the boundary of an Activity. *Normal flow* cannot be used for a *catch* Compensation Event. However, the *throw* Compensation Intermediate Event is used in *normal flow*.

The use of both *throwing* and *catching* versions of these Events are detailed in "Compensation and Transactions" on page 183.

Conditional Intermediate Events

The Conditional Intermediate Event represents a situation where a Process is waiting for a pre-defined *condition* to become *true*. This type of Event has a lined paper marker within the Event shape (see Figure 8-19, above).

Figure 8-54—A Conditional Intermediate Event

There are three ways to use Conditional Intermediate Events:

- In *normal flow*, but only as *catch* Events. Conditional Events are not *thrown*.
- Attached to an Activity boundary to interrupt it.
- As part of an Event-Based Gateway (see page 140).

This type of Event is triggered by a change in the data related to the Process. For example, a Conditional Intermediate Event might fire if a company's quarterly sales are 20 percent below the projection, or if the prevailing bank base rate changes. For a more detailed example and description of *conditions*, see "Conditional Start Events" on page 91.

It would be rare to use a Conditional Intermediate Event in *normal flow*, but it is possible. When a *token* arrives at the Event it will wait there until the Event is triggered (the *condition* becomes *true*). When the *condition* does become *true*, then the Process will continue. However, if the *condition* <u>never</u> becomes *true*, then the Process will become stuck at that point and will never complete normally.

In most cases, a Conditional Intermediate Event is attached to an Activity boundary so that the change of *condition* interrupts the Activity. See "Interrupting Activities with Events on page 99 for a general description of how Events interrupt Activities.

In BPMN 1.1, the Rule Intermediate Event was renamed the Conditional Intermediate Event as it represented a more accurate description of the behavior.

Link Intermediate Events

Link Intermediate Events are always used in pairs, with a *source* and a *target* Event (see Figure 8-55). Informally, we also call them Link Events. To ensure the pairing, both the *source* and *target* Link Events must have the same label. The *source* Link Event is a *throwing* Intermediate Event (with an arrow marker that has a black-colored fill) and the *target* Link Event is a *catching* Intermediate Event (with an arrow marker that has a white colored fill).

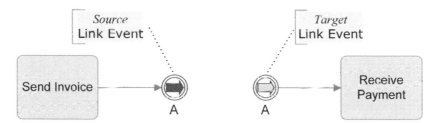

Figure 8-55—A virtual Sequence Flow is created

Using a pair of Link Events creates a *virtual* Sequence Flow. This means that the diagram in Figure 8-55 above, with the pair of Link Events between the two Activities, is equivalent to Figure 8-56, below, where a single Sequence Flow connects the Activities.

Figure 8-56—Equivalent behavior to paired Link Events

The scope of Link Events has changed in BPMN 1.1. As a result, Link Events are now only used as Intermediate Events and must exist within a single Process level. Link Events are no longer used for communicating between Processes or Process levels—Signal Events, which are new in BPMN 1.1, are used instead.

Link Events are used in two ways:

- 'Off-Page' Connectors
- 'Go-To' Objects

Link Intermediate Event Behavior

When a *token* arrives at a *source* Link Event (from the *incoming* Sequence Flow), the Event is triggered immediately (see Figure 8-57). Note that the distance between the Events is usually much greater than shown in the figure.

Figure 8-57—A *token* arrives at the *throw* Link Event

Once the *Source* Link Event is triggered (the *throw*), the *token* immediately jumps to the *catching (Target)* Link Event (see Figure 8-58). The arrival of the *token* at the *Target* Link Event immediately triggers the Event.

Figure 8-58—The *token* immediately jumps to the *catch* Link Event

After the *Target* Link Event is triggered, the *token* immediately moves down the Event's *outgoing* Sequence Flow (see Figure 8-59).

Figure 8-59—*Token* moving down the *outgoing* Sequence Flow

In keeping with idea that the paired Link Events act as a virtual Sequence Flow, the *token* travels down the Sequence Flow, jumps between the Events, and moves down the second Sequence Flow; all in the same time that it would take the *token* to travel down a single Sequence Flow (i.e., instantaneously).

Off-Page Connectors

Link Events can show how Sequence Flow continues from one page to another. Figure 8-60 displays a segment of a Process that can fit on one page. The far right side of the page has the first of a pair of Link Events that connects that segment of the Process to another segment of the Process on another page. Figure 8-61 shows the matching Link Event.

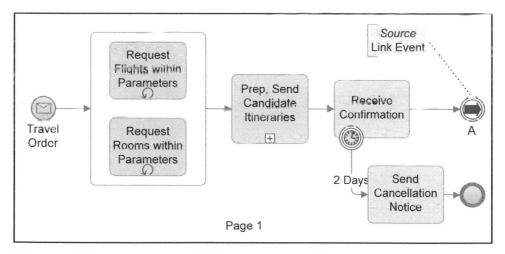

Figure 8-60—A *source* Link Events at the *end* of a printed page

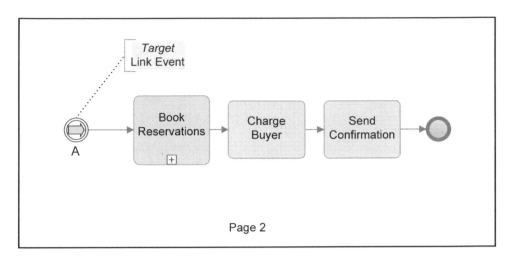

Page 2

Figure 8-61—A *target* Link Events at the *start* of a printed page

Between them, the pair of Link Events creates a *virtual* Sequence Flow that connects the last Activity on Page 1 ("Receive Confirmation") to the first Activity on Page 2 ("Book Reservations").

This is useful for printing diagrams or for methodologies where you have a limited number of objects on a page (e.g., IDEF limits the number of Activities to 5 or 6 per page).

Go-To Objects

Another way to use Link Events is as "Go-To Objects" (as in Figure 8-62).

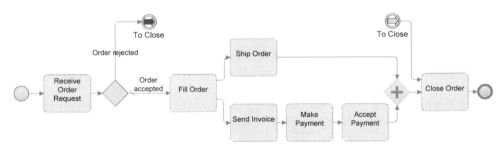

Figure 8-62—Link Events used as "Go-To" objects

The Process above contains an example of a flow that jumps from one Link Event to another. Generally, paired Link Events used in this way avoid very long Sequence Flow in diagrams (usually for diagrams that are much larger than this small example).

Link Events can direct the flow downstream, as in the example, or they can direct the flow back *upstream*, creating a loop. The only restriction is that the *virtual* Sequence Flow created must be a valid connection.

There can be <u>only one</u> *Target* Link Event, but there may be <u>multiple</u> *Source* Link Events paired with the same *catching* Link Event. There would be a separate virtual Sequence Flow for each of the *Source* Link Events.

Multiple Intermediate Events

The Multiple Intermediate Event uses the pentagon marker within the Event shape (see Figure 8-63). It represents a collection of any valid Intermediate Event *triggers*. However, the collection of *triggers* must be all *throwing* or all *catching* Events.

Figure 8-63—Multiple Intermediate Events

When *throwing* the collection of *triggers*, then the pentagon marker has a black fill. Link Intermediate Events, being a special case of paired Events, cannot be used in a Multiple Intermediate Event. Thus, the *triggers* that are valid for this type of Event are: Message, Compensation, and Signal. When a *token* arrives at the Event it fires (throws) <u>the entire set</u> of *triggers* in the collection.

When *catching* the collection of *triggers*, the pentagon marker has a white fill. <u>Any one</u> of the collection of *triggers* will trigger the Event.

The icon for the Multiple Intermediate Event has changed from a six-pointed star to a pentagon shape in BPMN 1.1 (as shown in Figure 8-63, above).

End Events

An End Event marks where a Process, or more specifically, a "path" within a Process, ends.[27] An End Event is a small, open circle with a single, thick lined boundary (see Figure 8-64).

---

[27] Paths are sometimes referred to as *threads*.

○

Figure 8-64—An End Event

Just like Start Events and Intermediate Events, there are different types of End Events that indicate different categories of *results* for the Process. A *result* is something that occurs at the end of a particular path of the Process (for example, a *message* is sent, or a *signal* is broadcast).

All End Events are *throw results* (i.e. it does not make sense to *catch* at the end of a Process). Thus, all the Event markers are black-filled. There are eight different types of End Events, each with its own graphical representation.

Again we have grouped them into *core* and *advanced* types:

Core End Events (see Figure 8-65):

- **None**—No *result* is defined.
- **Message**—Communication to another Business Entity (*participant* or Process).
- **Signal**—Defines a "broadcast" Event that any other Process can see and react to.
- **Terminate**—Stops <u>all</u> Process Activities, even if there are ongoing in other Threads (Parallel Paths).

Figure 8-65—Core types of End Events

Advanced Start Events (see Figure 8-66):

- **Error**—An end state that will disrupt the Process or require correction.
- **Cancel**—Used with the Transaction Sub-Process, this Event causes the cancellation of the Transaction Sub-Process. It is the *throw* for the *catch* that is on the Transac-

BPMN Modeling and Reference Guide

tion Sub-Process boundary (see Compensation and Transactions on page 183).

- **Compensation**—Also used as part of the Transaction Sub-Process behavior, this Event *throws* the undo *trigger* (in case the *instance* needs to be rolled-back). It can be linked to a specific Activity, or it can be left as a general Compensation event in which case it applies globally to this *instance*.

- **Multiple**—Defines two or more of Message, Error, Compensation, or Signal *results* (fires all *triggers*).

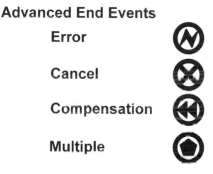

Advanced End Events

Error

Cancel

Compensation

Multiple

Figure 8-66—Advanced types of End Events

In BPMN 1.1, the Signal End Event replaces the Link End Event. The Signal Event is a more general way of communicating between or within Processes. This is a new Event type in BPMN 1.1. Also, the Event marker for the Multiple End Event changed in BPMN 1.1. Another addition in 1.1 was the inclusion of a global effect for the Compensation End Event.

Connecting End Events

End Events have a similar, but opposite, restriction for connections as do Start Events. Only <u>incoming</u> Sequence Flow is permitted—i.e. Sequence Flow cannot leave <u>from</u> an End Event—it can only arrive at an End Event (see Figure 8-67).

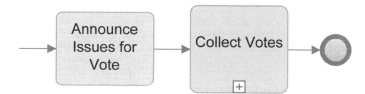

Figure 8-67—An End Event used in a Process

End Event Behavior

End Events represents where the flow of a Process ends, and thus, are where *tokens* are consumed. When a *token* arrives at an End Event, the *result* of the Event, if any, occurs and the *token* is consumed (see Figure 8-68).

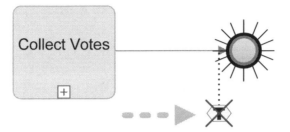

Figure 8-68—A *token* is consumed when it arrives at an End Event

The Process path completes as the *token* is consumed by the End Event. Of course, multiple End Events can appear within a Process (see Figure 8-69). Because of this, it is possible to have one or more paths (threads) that continue even after the *token* in one path has reached an End Event and has been consumed. If the Process still contains an unconsumed *token*, then the Process is still "active." After all active paths have reached an End Event, the Process is then complete. Note that some paths of a Process may not be traversed by a *token* during a specific performance of a Process.

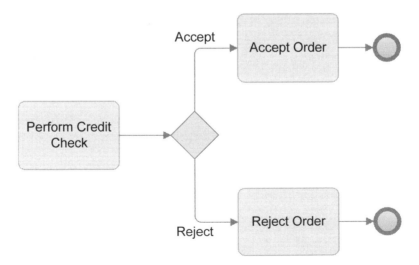

Figure 8-69—Multiple End Events in a Process

None End Events

An End Event without a *result* is known as a None End Event. Since there is no *result* defined, there is no marker in the center of the shape (see Figure 8-70). Also, a None End Event is <u>always</u> used to mark the end of Sub-Processes (moving from one level up to the next).

○

Figure 8-70—A None End

Message End Events

The Message End Event uses the envelope marker within the Event shape (see Figure 8-66, above). It indicates that the ending of a Process path results in the <u>sending</u> of a *message* to another *participant* or Process (i.e. it cannot communicate with a catching Message Intermediate Event in the same Pool). When a *token* reaches the *message* End Event, the *message* is sent and the *token* is consumed (see Figure 8-71).

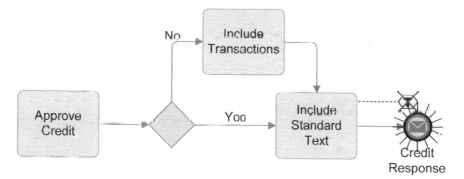

Figure 8-71—An Example of a Message End Event

Signal End Event

The Signal End Event uses a solid triangle marker within the Event shape (see Figure 8-72). It indicates that the end of a Process path results in the broadcast of a *signal*. When a *token* reaches the Signal End Event, it triggers the broadcast before consuming the *token*.

Figure 8-72—A Signal End Event

For more details on signals and how Signal Events are used, see "Using Signal Events" on page 112.

Terminate End Event

The Terminate End Event uses a black filled circle within the Event shape (see Figure 8-66, above). This End Event has a special characteristic, differentiating it from all the other types of End Events. The Terminate End Event will cause the immediate cessation of the Process *instance* at its current level and for any Sub-Processes (even if there is still ongoing activity), but it will not terminate a higher-level *parent* Process. Effectively, it ends the current *thread* and causes all other active *threads* to end immediately, regardless of their respective states.

Figure 8-73 provides one example of how a Terminate End Event is often used. In this Process, there are two parallel paths. The upper path is effectively an *infinite loop* that sends a *message* every seven days. When the lower path reaches the Terminate End Event the work of the upper path will be stopped, thereby stopping the *infinite loop*.

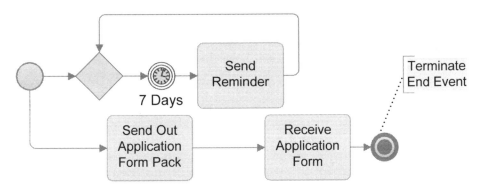

Figure 8-73—A Terminate End Event

Terminate End Events are used widely as they can facilitate a great deal of flexibility in combination with other BPMN features. For example, a separate thread might trigger non-interrupting escalations and alerts, but if the process completes in time (with the Terminate End Event); then the other thread never gets to fire. See Figure 8-36 on page 107 for an example.

Error End Event

The Error End Event represents a situation where the end of a Process path results in an *error*. This type of Event has a lightning bolt marker within the Event shape.

Figure 8-74 shows an example where an Error End Event is used. The *error* thrown by the Event will be caught by an Intermediate Event at a higher level (see Figure 8-75, below).

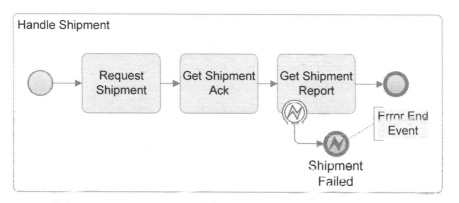

Figure 8 74—An Example of an Error End Event

In addition to the name of the Event, the definition of the *error* includes an *error code*. This error code is used by Events that are waiting to *catch* the *error*.

Unlike *signals*, *errors* are not broadcast throughout or across Processes. *Errors* have a specific scope of visibility. An *error* can only be seen by a *parent* Process. Other Processes at the same level or within different Pools cannot see the error. Errors only move upward in the Process hierarchy. If there happens to be more than one Process level higher than the Error End Event, then first level that has a *catch* Error Intermediate Event attached to its boundary will be interrupted, even if there are higher levels that could possible *catch* the same *error*.

Figure 8-75 shows how Error Intermediate Events attached to a Sub-Process boundary are used to catch *errors* thrown within internal activities. The *error* thrown by the End Event within the "Handle Shipment" Sub-Process (as shown in Figure 8-74, above) is caught by the "Shipment Failed" Error Intermediate Event.

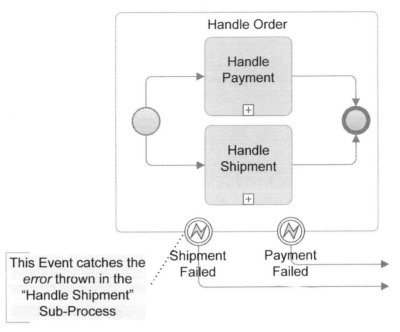

Handle Order

Handle
Payment

Handle
Shipment

This Event catches the
error thrown in the
"Handle Shipment"
Sub-Process

Shipment
Failed

Payment
Failed

Figure 8-75—Catching the *error* of an Error End Event

Note that the above Sub-Process has two different Error Intermediate Events attached to its border. Each one is designed to handle a different *error*.

Cancel End Event

The Cancel End Event uses an "X" marker within the Event shape
(see Figure 8-76). It indicates that the end of a Process path results in the cancellation of a Transaction Sub-Process.

Figure 8-76—A Cancel End Event

To *cancel* the Transaction Sub-Process, the Cancel End Event
must be contained within the Sub-Process or within a lower-level
child Sub-Process. See "Compensation and Transactions" on page
183 for more details on how Transaction Sub-Processes are cancelled.

Compensation End Event

The Compensation End Event indicates that the ending of a Process path results in the triggering of a *compensation*. It is distinguished from other types of End Events by the "rewind" symbol marker that is placed within the Event shape (see Figure 8-77).

Figure 8-77—A Compensation End Event

In the definition of the Compensation End Event the name of an Activity can be identified as the Activity that should be *compensated*. The Activity must be within the Process, either at the top-level Process or within a Sub-Process. If the named Activity was completed and it has an attached Compensation Intermediate Event, then that Activity will be *compensated* (see more about the "Compensation Intermediate Event" on page 118).

If an Activity is <u>not</u> identified in the definition of the Compensation End Event, then the resulting behavior is blanket *compensation*. All *completed* Activities within the Process *instance* that have an attached Compensation Intermediate Event are *compensated*.

An example of how *compensation* is handled is detailed in "Compensation and Transactions" on page 183.

Multiple End Event

The Multiple End Event uses a pentagon marker within the Event shape (see Figure 8-78). It represents a collection of two or more End Event *results*. The *results* can be any combination of *messages*, *errors*, *compensations*, and/or *signals*. When a *token* arrives at the Event it fires (throws) the entire set of *results* in the collection

Figure 8-78—A Multiple End Event

The icon for the Multiple End Event has changed from a six-pointed star to a pentagon shape in BPMN 1.1 (as shown in Figure 8-78).

Chapter 9.   Gateways

Gateways are modeling elements that control how the Process diverges <u>or</u> converges—i.e. they represent points of control for the paths within the Process. They split and merge the flow of a Process (through Sequence Flow). All Gateways share a diamond shape (see Figure 9-1).

Figure 9-1—A Gateway

The underlying idea is that Gateways are unnecessary if the Sequence Flow does not require controlling. Examples of controlling the flow include the alternative paths of a decision in the Process— e.g. take one path if "Yes" and the other if "No"; or waiting for two separate paths to reach a certain point before the Process can continue (a synchronization point). Both of these examples would use a Gateway to control the flow.

A Gateway *splits* the flow when it has multiple *outgoing* Sequence Flow and will *merge* the flow when it has multiple *incoming* Sequence Flow (see Figure 9-2). A single Gateway may have both multiple *incoming* and multiple *outgoing* Sequence Flow (i.e. both *merges* and *splits* at the same time).

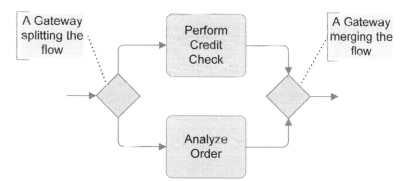

Figure 9-2—Gateways both *split* and *merge* the Process Flow

Since there are different ways of controlling the Process flow, there are different types of Gateways. While they all share the same basic shape footprint (a diamond), internal markers differentiate the behavior that each represents. The two most commonly used Gateways are Exclusive and Parallel. The Event Gateway is less commonly used (at this point), but we believe will become more important as modelers become more familiar (educated) with its capabilities.[28] These three Gateways make up the set of *core* Gateways (see Figure 9-3).

Core Gateways:

- **Exclusive**—*Splitting*: the Gateway will send a *token* down only <u>one</u> *outgoing* path (exclusively) depending on the evaluation of Sequence Flow *conditions*. *Merging*: the Gateway will "pass through" any *token* from any *incoming* paths.
- **Event**—*Splitting*: the Gateway sends a *token* down only one *outgoing* path (exclusively) depending on the occurrence of a specified Event (e.g., the arrival of a *message*). *Merging*: the Gateway will "pass through" any *token* from any *incoming* paths.
- **Parallel**—*Splitting*: the Gateway will send a *token* down <u>all</u> *outgoing* paths (in parallel). *Merging*: the Gateway will wait for a *token* from all *incoming* paths.

Core Gateways

Exclusive

Event

Parallel

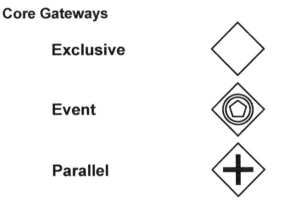

Figure 9-3—*Core* Gateways

The remaining two types of Gateways (Inclusive and Complex) make up our list of *advanced* Gateways (see Figure 9-4):

Advanced Gateways:

- **Inclusive**—*Splitting*: the Gateway will send a *token* down <u>one to all</u> *outgoing* paths (inclusively) depending on the evaluation of all Sequence Flow *conditions*. *Merging*: the Gateway will wait for a *token* from one to all *incoming* paths depending on which paths are expecting a *token*.

---

[28] Although the Event-Based Gateway is not widely used at present, we believe this is due to the fact that few people understand it. This is included in our *core* set as it is such a useful construct.

- **Complex**—*Splitting*: the Gateway will send a *token* down one to all *outgoing* paths (inclusively) depending on the evaluation of single Gateway *condition*. *Merging*: the Gateway will wait for a *token* from one to all *incoming* paths depending on the evaluation of a single Gateway *condition*.

Advanced Gateways

Inclusive

Complex

Figure 9-4—*Advanced* Gateways

The type (*splitting* and *merging*) for a single Gateway must be matched—i.e. a Gateway cannot be Parallel on the input side, and Exclusive on the output side. Note that *incoming* and *outgoing* Sequence Flow can connect to any point on the boundary of the Gateway. They are not required to connect to any predetermined points of the Gateway's diamond shape such as the corners of the diamond (although some vendors might impose this restriction in their modeling tools).

Four of the Gateways (Exclusive, Parallel, Inclusive, and Event) have pre defined behavior (i.e., ways of controlling the flow). The fifth type, the Complex Gateway, provides a way for a Modeler to specify (program) any desired behavior.

Exclusive Gateways

Exclusive Gateways are locations within a Process where there are two or more alternative paths. Think of them as a "fork in the road" of the Process—usually, they represent a decision. Like all Gateways, the Exclusive Gateway, uses a diamond shape. The criteria for the decision, which the Exclusive Gateway represents, exist as *conditions* on each of the *outgoing* Sequence Flow. Depending on the level of detail of the model, the *conditions* are defined as regular text (e.g., "Yes" or "No") or as *expressions* (e.g., "order_amount > $100,000.00").

Like all Gateways, Exclusive Gateways have an internal marker (an "X"). However, the display of this marker is optional and, in fact, the default presentation of the Exclusive Gateway is without the marker (see Figure 9-5). [29]

Figure 9-5—An Exclusive Gateway with, and without, an internal marker

Exclusive Gateway Splitting Behavior

Exclusive Gateways will split the flow when they have two or more *outgoing* paths. The Process (a *token*) will continue down only one of them. Thus, when considering *tokens*, even though multiple *outgoing* Sequence Flow exist, only <u>one</u> *token* is passed on through <u>one</u> of those Sequence Flow.

When a *token* arrives at an Exclusive Gateway (see Figure 9-6), there is an immediate evaluation of the *conditions* that are on the Gateway's *outgoing* Sequence Flow. One of those *conditions* <u>must</u> always evaluate to *true*.

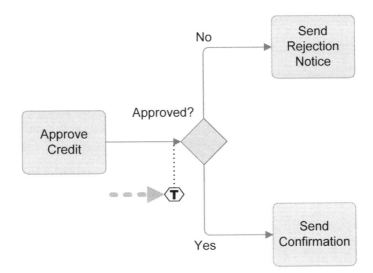

Figure 9-6—A *token* arrives at an Exclusive Gateway and is directed down one of the *outgoing* Sequence Flow

The evaluation of the Sequence Flow *conditions* is actually done one at a time, in the order that they are listed in the attributes of

---

[29] All of the Process examples in this book will use the Exclusive Gateway <u>without</u> the internal marker.

the Gateway (not necessarily in any arbitrary order they are displayed on the diagram). The *token* moves down the <u>first</u> Sequence Flow with the *condition* that evaluates to *true*. So if more than one *condition* happens to be *true*, then after the first one identified, the Gateway will ignore any remaining *true conditions*—it never evaluates them. Use an <u>Inclusive</u> Gateway if the Process needs to activate more than one *outgoing* Sequence Flow (see page 148).

The *condition* that evaluates to *true* is often different each time the Process is performed, or each time the *conditions* for an Exclusive Gateway are evaluated (e.g., if the Gateway is part of a loop). For example, in Figure 9-7, if the *condition* for the lower *outgoing* Sequence Flow ("Yes") from the Gateway is *true*, then the *token* will be sent down that path.

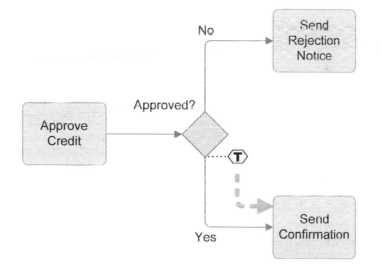

Figure 9-7—An Exclusive Gateway Using *conditions* to Branch the Sequence Flow

Perhaps the next time a *token* reaches the Exclusive Gateway, the *condition* for the upper *outgoing* Sequence Flow ("No") is *true* and the *token* moves down that path.

As we mentioned above, one of *conditions* in the *outgoing* Sequence Flow <u>must</u> evaluate to *true*. This means that the modeler should define the *conditions* to meet this requirement. If the *conditions* are complicated, it might not be obvious that at least one *condition* will be *true* for all performances of the Process. If it does turn out that none of the *conditions* are *true*, then the Process will be stuck at the Gateway and will not complete normally.

Use a default condition—*One way for the modeler to ensure that the Process does not get stuck at an Exclusive Gateway is to use a* default condition *for one of the* outgoing *Sequence Flow (see Figure 9-8). This creates a Default Sequence Flow (see "Default Sequence Flow" on page 172). The Default is chosen if* <u>*all*</u> *the other Sequence Flow conditions* turn out to be *false.*

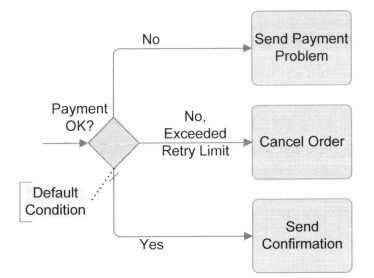

Figure 9-8—An Exclusive Gateway with a Default Sequence Flow

Exclusive Gateway Merging Behavior

Exclusive Gateways can also merge Sequence Flow. That is, they can have multiple *incoming* Sequence Flow. However, When a *token* arrives at the Exclusive Gateway, there is no evaluation of *conditions* (on the *incoming* Sequence Flow), nor is there any synchronization of *tokens* that might happen to come down any other of the *incoming* Sequence Flow. The *token*, when it arrives, immediately moves down the *outgoing* Sequence Flow. Effectively, there is an immediate "pass-through" of the *token* (see Figure 9-9).

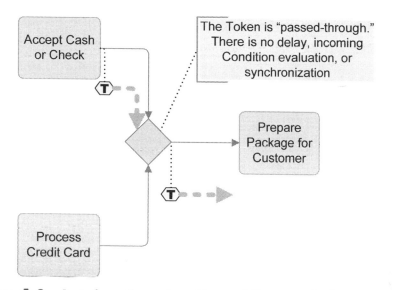

Figure 9-9—A *token* "passing-through" one of the *Incoming* Sequence Flow for an Exclusive Gateway

Note that when the Exclusive Gateway has only one *outgoing* Sequence Flow, then that Sequence Flow will not have a *condition*. If the Gateway also has multiple *outgoing* Sequence Flow, then the Sequence Flow will have *conditions* to be evaluated as described in the section above.

If another *token* arrives from another *incoming* Sequence Flow, then it will also pass straight through, triggering the *outgoing* Sequence Flow again—i.e., there will be two *instances* of the Prepare Package for Customer in Figure 9-9, above.

Most of the time, a modeler will probably not need to worry about this behavior as a *branching (splitting)* Exclusive Gateway normally precedes the *merge*. In such circumstances, only one *token* will arrive at the *merge* anyway. Sometimes it will come down one path and sometimes down the other.

On the other hand, there may be situations where there are (potentially) multiple *tokens* arriving at a Gateway. In such circumstances, if the desired behavior is that only the first *token* should pass through (ignoring the rest), then a Complex Gateway is needed (see Figure 9-32 on page 155).

The behavior of the other types of Gateways usually includes waiting for (synchronizing) other *tokens* from other *incoming* Sequence Flow (as we shall discuss later), but Exclusive Gateways do not.

Event-Based Exclusive Gateways

Event-Based Exclusive Gateways represent an alternative branching point where the decision is based on <u>two or more Events</u> that might occur, rather than data-oriented *conditions* (as in an Exclusive Gateway). We will often use "Event Gateway," when referring to this Gateway. Since more than one Event controls the Event-Based Gateway, the marker within the diamond is the same as the Multiple Intermediate Event (a pentagon surrounded by two concentric circles—see Figure 9-10).

Figure 9-10—An Event Gateway

Processes that involve communications with a business partner or some external entity often need this sort of behavior. For example, if the business partner sends a *message* that says "Yes, let's do it" the Process would head off down one path. If, on the other hand, the business partner sends a *message* that says "No thanks" the Process needs to head off down a different path. And if the business partner did not respond, a Timer is required to avoid the Process becoming deadlocked. Event-Based Gateways allow this sort of flexibility. Several examples of Event-Based Gateways are used in the introductory chapters such as those shown in Figure 5-7 on page 46 and Figure 5-12 on page 56.

Note that the marker for the Exclusive Event Gateway has changed in BPMN 1.1. This is because the Gateway marker is a Multiple Intermediate Event, which has changed to a pentagon from a six-pointed star).

Event Gateway Splitting Behavior

The Event Gateway is unique in BPMN in that its normal behavior is actually determined by a combination of *flow objects*. The Gateway by itself is not sufficient to accomplish the exclusive *splitting* of the flow. The Event Gateway also uses a combination of Intermediate Events to create the behavior. These Events, which must be of the *catch* variety, are the first objects connected by the Gateway's *outgoing* Sequence Flow (see Figure 9-11—the Group surrounding the configuration of the Gateway provides emphasis).

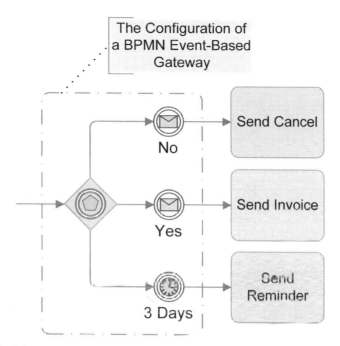

Figure 9-11—An Event Gateway configuration (with an added Group for emphasis)

The following *catch* Intermediate Events are valid in an Event Exclusive Gateway:

- Message
- Timer
- Conditional
- Signal

Receive Tasks may also be used in place of Message Intermediate Events. However, you cannot mix the two (Message Intermediate Events and Receive Tasks).

When the *token* arrives at the Gateway (see Figure 9-12) it will immediately pass-through the Gateway and then split up sending one *token* to each of the Events that follow the Gateway (see Figure 9-13).

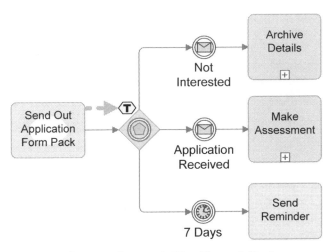

Figure 9-12—A *token* arrives at the Event Gateway

Since all the Intermediate Events are catch Events, the *tokens* will wait there until one of the Events is triggered.

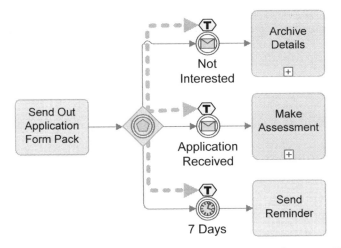

Figure 9-13—The *token* is split and sent down all of the Gateway's *outgoing* Sequence Flow

The situation here is similar to Activity with attached Intermediate Events (see "Interrupting Activities with Events" on page 99). The Intermediate Events that are part of the Gateway configuration become involved in a *race condition*. Whichever one finishes first (fires) will win the *race* and take control of the Process with its *token*. Then the *token* will immediately continue down its *outgoing* Sequence Flow (from that Intermediate Event—see Figure 9-14). The *tokens* waiting in the other Events are immediately consumed, disabling those paths.

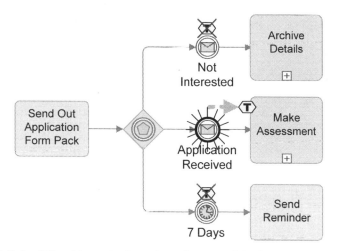

Figure 9-14—The Event that is triggered "chooses" the path

There is always a risk that the Events chosen for the Event Gateway configuration may not occur for a given Process *instance*. If none of the Events are triggered, for whatever reason, then the Process will become stuck at the Gateway and will not complete normally. If none of the other Events trigger, then the *timer* will eventually fire, allowing the Process to continue (and to deal with why the other Events never happened).

Best Practice: **Use a Timer Intermediate Event with an Event Gateway**—*One way for the modeler to ensure that the Process does not get stuck at an Event Based Exclusive Gateway is to use a* Timer Intermediate Event *as one of the options for the Gateway (see Figure 9-11, above).*

Event Gateway Merging Behavior

Unlike all the other Gateways, the Event Gateway is <u>always</u> used to *split* the Process flow. However, at the same time, they *merge* Process flow. The merging behavior of the Event Gateway is exactly the same as the merging behavior of the Exclusive Gateway (see "Exclusive Gateway Merging Behavior" on page 138).

Parallel Gateways

Parallel Gateways insert a split in the Process to create two or more parallel paths (threads). They can also merge parallel paths. The "+" marker is used to identify this type of Gateway (see Figure 9-15).

Figure 9-15—A *Parallel* Gateway

Parallel Gateway Splitting

Parallel Gateways will split the flow when they have two or more *outgoing* paths. When a *token* arrives at a Parallel Gateway (see Figure 9-16), there is no evaluation of any *conditions* on the *outgoing* Sequence Flow (unlike the Exclusive Gateway).

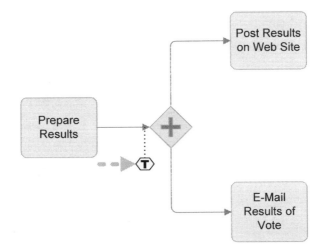

Figure 9-16—A single *token* arriving at a Parallel Gateway

By definition, the Parallel Gateway will create parallel paths. This means that the Gateway will create a number of *tokens* that are equal to the number of *outgoing* Sequence Flow. One *token* moves down <u>each</u> of those *outgoing* Sequence Flow (see Figure 9-17). There is no delay between the arrival of the *token* to the Gateway and the *tokens* leaving the Gateway.

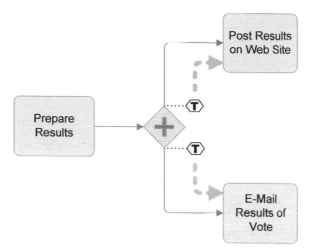

Figure 9-17—Two *tokens* leaving a Parallel Gateway

Parallel Gateway Merging

Use a merging Parallel Gateway when parallel paths require syn-chronization before the Process can continue. To synchronize the flow, the Parallel Gateway will wait for a *token* to arrive from <u>each</u> *incoming* Sequence Flow. When the first *token* arrives, there is no evaluation of a *condition* for the *incoming* Sequence Flow, but the *token* is "held" at the Gateway and does not continue (see Figure 9-18).

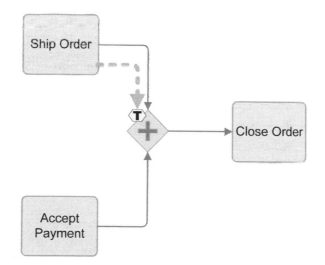

Figure 9-18—A Parallel Gateway *merging* the Sequence Flow

This "holding" of *tokens* will continue until a *token* arrives from <u>all</u> *incoming* Sequence Flow (see Figure 9-19)

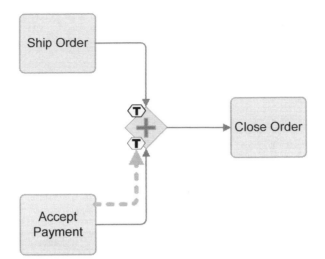

Figure 9-19—*tokens* are *merged* at the Parallel Gateway

When <u>all</u> the *tokens* have arrived, then they are merged and one *token* moves down the *outgoing* Sequence Flow (see Figure 9-20).

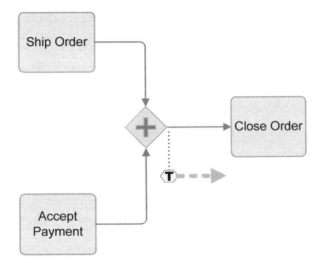

Figure 9-20—The *token* can move on once all *incoming tokens* are received

If there is more than one *outgoing* Sequence Flow emanating from a *merging* Parallel Gateway, then each will receive a *token* when all *incoming* Sequence Flow have arrived. Effectively, this will create another set of parallel threads.

BPMN Modeling and Reference Guide

Best Practice: **Ensure that the number of incoming *Sequence Flow is correct for a Parallel Gateway*—**The key point is to exercise care, ensuring that merging Parallel Gateways have the correct number of incoming Sequence Flow—especially when used in conjunction with other Gateways. As a guide, modelers should match merging and splitting Parallel Gateways (if the desired behavior is to merge them again).[30]

If the number of *incoming* Sequence Flow does not match with the number of *tokens* that will actually arrive, then the Process will get stuck at the Parallel Gateway, waiting for a *token* that never materializes —i.e., the Process can never complete properly. Figure 9-21 provides an example of such a Process configuration.

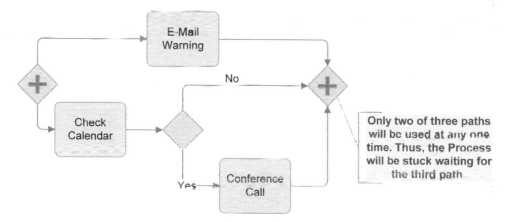

Figure 9-21—An example of <u>incorrect</u> use of a *Merging* Parallel Gateway

The correct way to model this situation shown is Figure 9-22. It involves placing an Exclusive Gateway prior to the merging Parallel Gateway to reduce the number of *incoming* Sequence Flow (in this case, down to two).

---

[30] Of course, it is possible to split the flow at a Parallel Gateway and never have the threads recombine. Ultimately each thread will finish at an End Event.

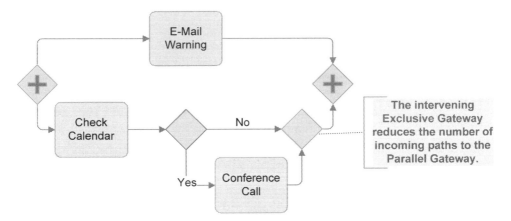

Figure 9-22—Matching the numbers of inputs on a *merging* Parallel Gateway

Inclusive Gateways

Inclusive Gateways support decisions where more than one out-come is possible at the decision point. The "O" marker identifies this type of Gateway (see Figure 9-23).

Figure 9-23—An Inclusive Gateway

Inclusive Gateway Splitting Behavior

Like the Exclusive Gateway, an Inclusive Gateway with multiple *outgoing* Sequence Flow creates alternative paths based on the *conditions* on those Sequence Flow. The difference is that the Inclusive Gateway activates <u>one or more</u> paths;[31] whereas the Exclusive Gateway will only activate <u>one</u> *outgoing* Sequence Flow and the Parallel Gateway will activate <u>all</u> *outgoing* Sequence Flow.

When a *token* arrives at an Inclusive Gateway (see Figure 9-24), there is an immediate evaluation of all the *conditions* that are on the Gateway's *outgoing* Sequence Flow.

---

[31] There is another mechanism for creating an inclusive split. This is achieved using multiple outgoing Conditional Sequence Flow from an Activity (see Conditional Sequence Flow on page 170).

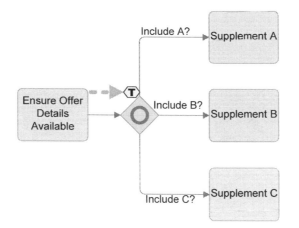

Figure 9-24—A *token* arrives at an Inclusive Gateway

Every *condition* that evaluates to *true* will result in a *token* moving down that Sequence Flow. As with the Exclusive Gateway, at least one of those *conditions* <u>must</u> evaluate to *true*. This means that any combination of Sequence Flow, from one of them to all of them, may receive a *token* each time the Gateway is used. In Figure 9-25, if the *condition* for the upper *outgoing* Sequence Flow ("Include A?") and the *condition* for the lower *outgoing* Sequence Flow ("Include B?") are *true*, then *tokens* move down both of those paths.

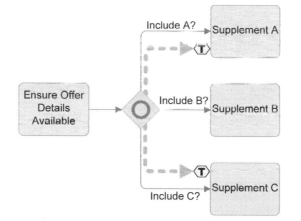

Figure 9-25—A *token* is directed down one or more of the *outgoing* Sequence Flow

Another time a *token* reaches the Exclusive Gateway, it might decide that the *condition* for the middle *outgoing* Sequence Flow ("Include B?") is the only one that evaluates to *true*, leading to a *token* moving down that path.

As described for the behavior of the *splitting* Exclusive Gateway, above (see page 136), one of *conditions* in the *outgoing* Sequence Flow <u>must</u> evaluate to *true* or the Process will be stuck at the Gateway and will not complete normally.

Best Practice: **Use a default condition**—*One way for the modeler to ensure that the Process does not get stuck at an Inclusive Gateway is to use a* default condition *for one of the outgoing Sequence Flow. This Default Sequence Flow will always evaluate to* true *if <u>all</u> the other Sequence Flow conditions turn out to be* false *(see "Default Sequence Flow" on page 172).*

Inclusive Gateway Merging Behavior

The *merging* behavior of the Inclusive Gateway is one of the more complex parts of BPMN to understand. The Gateway will synchronize the flow of the Process like the Parallel Gateway (see page 145), but it does so in a way that mirrors the output of the *splitting* Inclusive Gateway. That is, the Gateway will synchronize from <u>one to all</u> of the Gateway's *incoming* Sequence Flow. The Gateway will determine how many paths are expected to have a *token*.

We walk through an example to show how the Inclusive Gateway does this synchronization. When the first *token* arrives at the Gateway (see Figure 9-26), the Gateway will "look" *upstream* for each of the other *incoming* Sequence Flow to see if there is a *token* that might arrive at a later time. In the figure, there is another *token* in the bottom path still in the "Supplement C" Task, but there is no *token* in the middle path (in the "Supplement B" Task or further *upstream*).

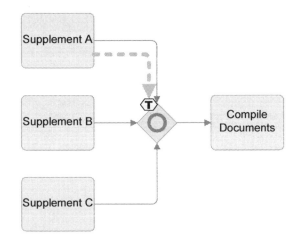

Figure 9-26—A *token* arrives at an Inclusive Gateway

Thus, the Gateway will hold the first *token* that arrived in the upper path until the other *token* from the lower path arrives (see Figure 9-27).

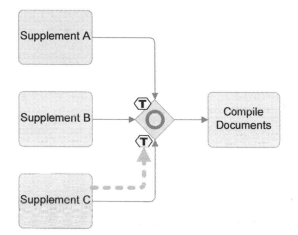

Figure 9-27—A second *token* arrives at an Inclusive Gateway, synchronizing the flow

When all the expected *tokens* have arrived at the Gateway, the Process flow is synchronized (the *incoming tokens* are *merged*) and then a *token* moves down the Gateway's *outgoing* Sequence Flow (see Figure 9-28).

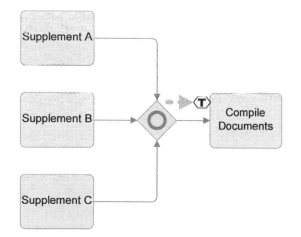

Figure 9-28—The *token* is sent down the *outgoing* Sequence Flow

Figure 9-29 shows a different *instance* of the Gateway where a *token* arrives from the middle path while there are no other *tokens* waiting *upstream* on either the upper or lower path. In this case, the *token* would immediately move down the *outgoing* Sequence Flow (as in Figure 9-28, above).

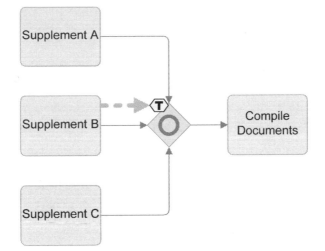

Figure 9-29—A *token* arrives at an Inclusive Gateway that does not need synchronization

Note that when the Inclusive Gateway has only one *outgoing* Sequence Flow, then that Sequence Flow will not have a *condition*. If the Gateway also has multiple *outgoing* Sequence Flow, then the Sequence Flow will have *conditions* to be evaluated as described in the section above.

An Inclusive Gateway that *merges* the flow is usually married up with a corresponding *splitting* Inclusive Gateway. When used in pairs in this way, the *splitting* Gateway will continue the flow down one to all paths and the *merging* Gateway will synchronize (wait for) all the paths that were generated for that *instance*.

Of course, it is possible to create Processes that include different combinations of *splitting* and *merging* Inclusive Gateways. In some cases, it will be hard to determine the pairing of the Gateways. It is difficult to make a Process deadlock (get stuck) when using Inclusive Gateways, but the actual behavior of the Process might not be what the modeler expects. So exercise caution when using merging Inclusive Gateways.[32]

Best Practice: ***Always use Inclusive Gateways in pairs**—A way to avoid unexpected behavior is to create models where a merging Inclusive*

---

[32] The general guideline used in the development of BPMN was to develop a modeling capability that did not constrain users too tightly, making the notation as flexible as possible. As a result, careless modeling can lead to problems.

Gateway follows a splitting Inclusive Gateway and that the number of Sequence Flow match between them (see Figure 9-30).

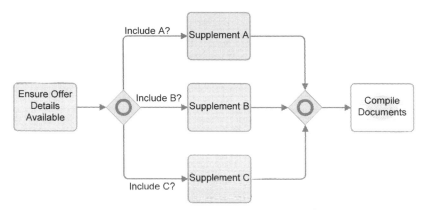

Figure 9-30—Inclusive Gateways that are paired for splitting and merging Sequence Flow

Complex Gateways

Complex Gateways use a bold asterisk as the marker shape within the diamond (see Figure 9-31). They are part of BPMN to handle situations where the other types of Gateways do not provide support for the desired behavior.

Figure 9-31—A Complex Gateway

Modelers provide their own expressions that determine the merging and/or splitting behavior of the Gateway. They often replace a set of standard Gateways, combining them into a single, more compact Gateway.

Complex Gateway Splitting Behavior

The splitting behavior of the Complex Gateway is the least interesting side of the Gateway. It is similar to the behavior of the Inclusive Gateway splitting behavior. The difference is that the Complex Gateway uses a single *outgoing assignment* within the Gateway, rather than a set of separate *conditions* on the *outgoing* Sequence Flow. The result is the same in that Gateway activates one or more of the *outgoing* paths (see "Inclusive Gateway Splitting Behavior" on page 148 for an example of this type of behavior).

An *assignment* has two parts: a *condition* and an *action*. When an *assignment* is performed, it evaluates the *condition* and if *true*, it then performs the *action* such as updating the value of a Process or Data Object property. In the case of a Complex Gateway, the *outgoing assignment* may send a *token* down one or more of the Gateway's *outgoing* Sequence Flow. The *outgoing assignment* may refer to data of the Process or its Data Objects and the status of the *incoming* Sequence Flow (i.e., is there a *token* there). For example, an *outgoing assignment* may evaluate Process data and then select different sets of *outgoing* Sequence Flow, based on the results of the evaluation. However, the *outgoing assignment* should ensure that at least one of the *outgoing* Sequence Flow will always be chosen.

Complex Gateway Merging Behavior

The more interesting side of the Complex Gateways is its *merging* behavior. There are many patterns that can be performed with the Complex Gateway, such as typical Inclusive Gateway behavior, batching of multiple *tokens*, accepting *tokens* from some paths but ignoring the *tokens* from others, etc. The Gateway looks the same for each of these patterns, so the modeler should use a Text Annotation to inform the reader of the diagram how it is used.

Best Practice: **Use a Text Annotation with the Complex Gateway**—*Since the actual behavior of a Complex Gateway will vary for each usage of the Gateway, use a Text Annotation to tell the reader of the diagram what behavior the Gateway is set to perform (see Figure 9-32).*

The Complex Gateway uses an *incoming assignment* when *tokens* arrive. The *condition* of the *incoming assignment* may refer to Process or Data Object information and the status of the *incoming* Sequence Flow. If the *condition* is *false*, nothing happens other than the *token* is held there. If the *condition* is *true*, then the *action* could be set to pass the *token* to the output side of the Gateway, thereby activating the *outgoing* assignment, or the *action* could be set to consume the *token*.

Of the many ways of using a Complex Gateway, we will use the discriminator pattern as a demonstration. In this pattern, there are two or more parallel activities. When one of the Activities completes, then the follow-on Activities can begin, but it does not matter which Activity completes. This is another example of a *race condition.* All the remaining Activities will complete normally, but they no longer have an impact on the Process flow.

In Figure 9-32, the "Start Analysis" Task should start after "Test A" or "Test B," it does not matter which one finishes first. But, after the second one finishes, the "Start Analysis" Task should <u>not</u> start again. In contrast, if the modeler chose an Exclusive Gateway to merge the flow, the "Start Analysis" Task would start again (i.e., two *instances*).

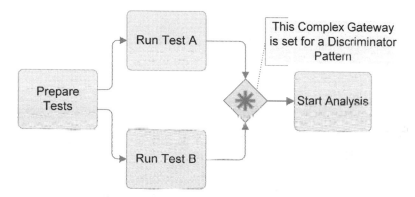

Figure 9-32—A Complex Gateway Merging the Sequence Flow

If the "Run Test A" Task completes first, its *token* is sent to the Gateway while the other *token* is still in the "Run Test B" Task (see Figure 9-33).

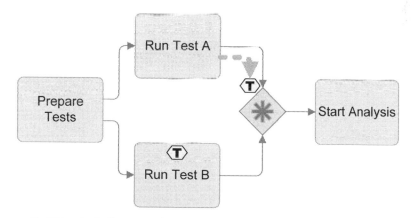

Figure 9-33—A *token* arrives at a Complex Gateway

For this pattern, the first *token* that arrives is immediately sent out down the *outgoing* Sequence Flow to the next Activity (see Figure 9-34).

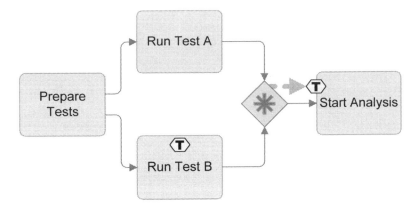

Figure 9-34—The first *token* passes through the Complex Gateway

When the other *token* finally arrives, it is consumed by the Gateway (see Figure 9-35)

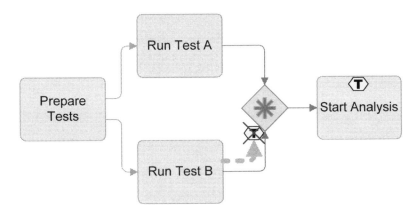

Figure 9-35—The second *token* is stopped at the Complex Gateway

Chapter 10. Swimlanes

BPMN uses "swimlanes" to help partition and/organize activities in a diagram. There are two main types:

- **Pools**—act as containers for a Process, each one representing a *participant* in a collaborative Business Process Diagram.
- **Lanes**—often assumed to represent internal business roles within a Process, Lanes actually provide a generic mechanism for partitioning the objects within a Pool based on the characteristics of the Process or elements.

Pools

The term "Pool" was derived by extending the swimlane analogy. A swimming pool has lanes. BPMN has two types of swimlane partitions and one type is included in the other. Thus, it made sense to call the sub-partitions Lanes and, the partition that contained the Lanes, a Pool.

In BPMN, Pools represent *participants* in an interactive or collaborative Business Process Diagram. A *participant* is defined as a general business role, e.g. a buyer, seller, shipper, or supplier. Alternatively, it could define a specific business entity, e.g. FedEx as the shipper. Each Pool can only represent <u>one</u> *participant*.

Pools are depicted as a rectangle box that acts as a container for the *flow objects* of a *participant's* Process. The Business Process Diagram referred to here is really a *collaboration,* detailing how the *participants* coordinate their behavior. *Participants* might have an abstract representation (e.g., "Buyer" or "Seller" *role*) or they may represent a distinct business *entity* (e.g., "IBM" or "Amazon.com").[33]

Since a BPMN diagram can depict the Processes of different *participants*, each *participant* may view the diagram differently. That is, each *participant* will have a different point of view—some Activities are under their control, while other Pools are external to them.

In practice, each Pool represents a distinct Process and each *participant* has its own Pool. A Pool is not required to contain a Proc-

---

[33] The term "*Participant*" references business-to-business collaborators who are each in charge of their own Processes. It does not refer to the roles or job titles of an organization.

ess. Known as a *"black box,"* these Pools do not show Activities or Sequence Flow inside its boundary. Figure 10-1, which was used in Part I of this book, shows a "Mortgage Company" Pool containing a Process and a "Customer" Pool whose Process is a *black box* (as far as Mortgage Co is concerned, they have no knowledge of the Processes of their Customer). When the Pool is a *black box* the Pool's shape can be sized and positioned in a way that is convenient for the modeler (that is, they do not have to extend the entire length of the diagram.

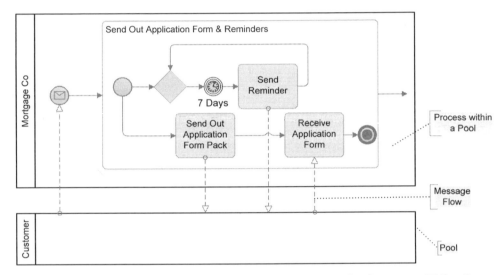

Figure 10-1—A *collaboration* with two Pools (one a *"black box"*)

Message Flow handle <u>all interactions</u> between Pools (and their Processes). When the Pool is *black box,* Message Flow connects to its boundary. Where a Pool has Process elements, the Message Flow connects to those elements (see Figure 10-1, above).

As discussed in the section on Sequence Flow on page 169, Sequence Flow cannot cross a Pool boundary—i.e., a Process is fully contained within a Pool. For a discussion on why Message Flow is used to synchronize the Processes between Participants see page 173.

In some cases, when the point of view of the diagram is clear, the boundary of the "main" Pool is not displayed. For example, the modelers for the "Mortgage Co" *participant* shown in Figure 10-1 above have developed the diagram and may not want to display the boundary of their Pool to emphasize the difference between internal and external *participants* (see Figure 10-2).

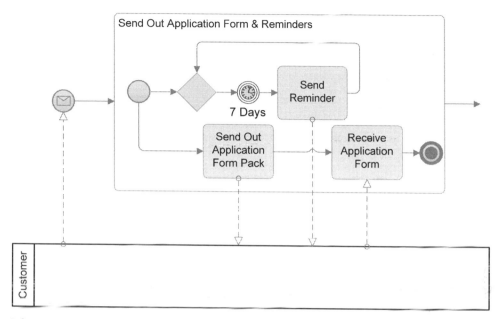

Figure 10-2—A diagram where the boundary of one Pool is not shown

Lanes

Lanes create sub-partitions for the objects within a Pool (see Figure 10-3). Theoc partitions are used to group Process elements (showing how they are related), or which roles have responsibility for carrying out the Activities.

Lanes often represent organization roles (e.g., Manager, Administration, Associate, etc), but can represent any desired classification (e.g., underlying technology, organizational departments, company products, location, etc).

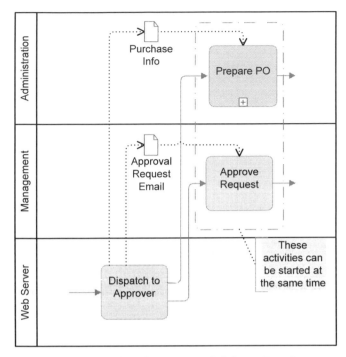

Figure 10-3—An example of Lanes within a Pool

It is also possible to nest Lanes (see Figure 10-4 where the "Marketing" Lane is sub-divided into the "Pre-Sales" and "Post-Sales").

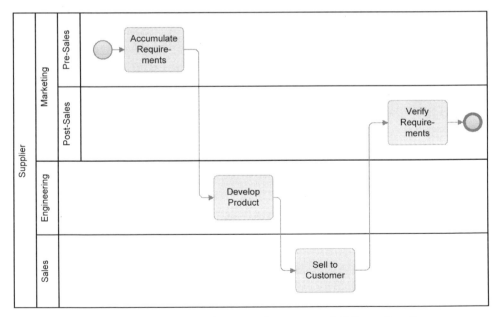

Figure 10-4—An example of nested Lanes within a Pool

The key points to remember about Lanes are:

- In BPMN 1.1 Lanes can represent any logical grouping (not just roles).[34] For example, Lanes can represent functional areas, business systems, business classifications (e.g., customer oriented, support oriented, etc), business locations, etc.
- Sequence Flow can cross Lane boundaries.
- Lanes can be nested.
- Message Flow is not used within or across Lanes of a Pool.[35]

[34] It is likely that this will be tightened up in BPMN 2.0.

[35] For a wider discussion on the reasons for this, see Message Flow on page 173.

Chapter 11.   Artifacts

Artifacts provide a mechanism to capture additional information about a Process, beyond the underlying flow-chart structure. This information does not directly impact the flow chart characteristics of a Process.

There are three standard Artifacts in BPMN:

- **Data Objects**—Used to represent the documents and data that are manipulated by Processes. Think of them as representing the "payload" of the Process.
- **Groups**—Provide a mechanism to highlight and categorize a section of the model or a set of Objects.
- **Text Annotations**—Add further descriptive information to a model (as an aid to understanding).

A modeler or tool can extend BPMN by defining new Artifacts; the only restriction is that they must have their own distinct shape and not conflict with the way existing shapes look and/or are configured.

Data Objects

Data Objects represent the data and documents in a Process. Data Objects use a standard document shape (rectangle with one corner bent over—see Figure 11-1).

Figure 11-1—A Data Object

Data Objects usually define the *inputs* and *outputs* of Activities. While Data Objects do not affect the structure and flow of the Process, they are intimately tied to *performance* of Activities. Associations indicate their direction (*input* or *output*) (see Figure 11-2). We will discuss the use of Data Objects and their relationship to Activities in more detail in "Data Flow" on page 176.

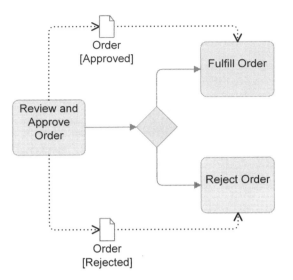

Figure 11-2—Data Objects are used for Data and Documents

Data Objects also have "*states*" that depict how the object (document) is updated within the Process. The *state* is usually shown under the name of the Data Object and is placed between brackets (as Figure 11-2, above, shows the "Order" Data Object with the *states* of "Approved" or "Rejected").

Figure 11-2 also illustrates a unique feature of Data Objects. The same Data Object can appear multiple times in a diagram. If the "Fulfill Order" Task appeared twice in the diagram, that would represent two separate *instances* of that Task. However, although the "Order" Data Object appears twice, it represents two representations of the <u>same</u> document.

By using the *state* of a Data Object and placing it within multiple locations within a diagram, the modeler can document the changes that a Data Object will go through during the Process.

Groups

A Group is a dashed, rounded rectangle used to surround a group of *flow objects* in order to highlight and/or categorize them. A long dash and a dot make up the line (see Figure 11-3).

Figure 11-3—A Group shape

Groups enclose a section of a model but do not add additional constraints on Process performance –as a Sub-Process would (Sequence Flow can pass through a Group boundary). It is merely a useful graphical mechanism for categorizing objects. Sequence Flow and Message Flow move through Group boundaries transparently. While Groups do not affect process performance, they can acts as a container for reporting.

Figure 11-4 shows a Group across two Pools. The Activities shown are related even though they are performed by different *participants* within different Pools.

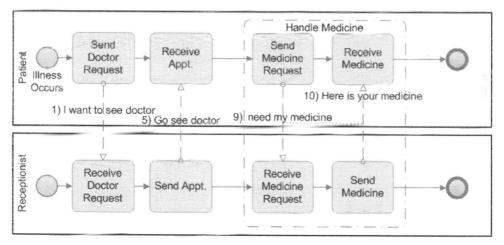

Figure 11-4—Groups graphically highlight any set or category of BPMN elements

Groups do not affect the flow of the Process and are not part of a Process decomposition. Although the Group will graphically highlight a set of Activities, this Group cannot be interrupted in the same way as a Sub-Process (see Figure 11-5 for an <u>incorrect</u> example). It is not possible to attach Intermediate Events to the boundary of a Group.

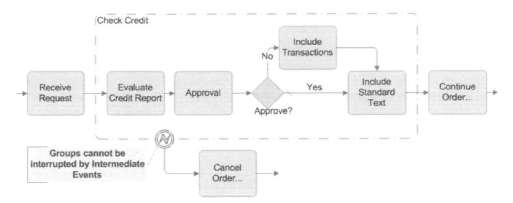

Figure 11-5—Incorrect use of a Group (it is not possible to attach Intermediate Events to a Group)

The correct way to interrupt the Activities in the figure above is to use a Sub-Process and then attach the Intermediate Event to the boundary as in Figure 11-6.

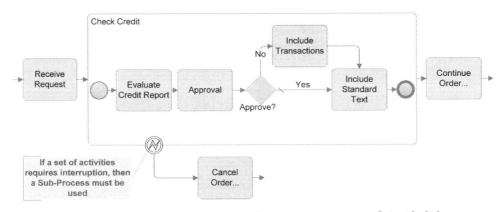

Figure 11-6—The Correct way to interrupt a set of Activities

Underpinning the Group element is the *category* concept (which is a common attribute to all BPMN elements). For example, Activities could be categorized, for analysis purposes, as "customer valued" or "business valued." A Group is merely a visual depiction of a single *category*. The graphical elements within the Group are assigned the *category* attribute linked to the Group. It is worth noting that *categories* might use other highlighting mechanisms, such as color, as defined by a modeler or a modeling tool. They could also support reporting or analysis (or any other purpose). Since a *category* is also a BPMN element, a *category* can have *categories*, creating a hierarchical structure (of *categories*).

Text Annotations

Text Annotations provide the modeler with the ability to add further descriptive information or notes about a Process or its elements. Text Annotations can connect to any object on the diagram or they can float freely anywhere on a diagram. The text for the Text Annotation is accompanied by an open box that can appear on either side of the text (see Figure 11-7).

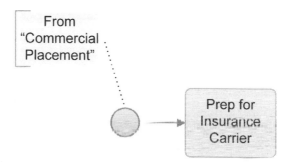

Figure 11-7—An Example of a Text Annotation

The line used to connect a Text Annotation to another object is an Association (see "Association" on page 174).

Note that Text Annotations feature throughout this book to provide descriptions and aid understanding of the examples and concepts presented.

Artifacts are Extendable

Modelers and tool vendors can extend BPMN through the addition of new types of Artifacts. Modeling tools may include features to hide, or show these Artifacts. Either way, the structure of the Process (the *flow objects* connected by Sequence Flow) will remain the same.

As with other Artifacts, these extensions cannot form part of the *normal flow* of Activities, Events, and Gateways—that is, Sequence Flow cannot directly connect to or from Artifacts. This was to ensure that BPMN diagrams always have a consistent and recognizable structure (i.e., aiding understanding) and to guarantee a consistent behavior of BPMN diagrams.

For example, a database or datastore might be represented by a cylinder graphic (see Figure 11-8). While this is not a standard BPMN Artifact, a modeler might add it.

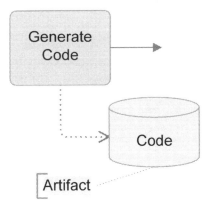

Figure 11-8—New Artifacts can be created by Modelers or Tool Vendors

Furthermore, specific industries or markets might develop their own sets of Artifacts. For example, practitioners in the telecom, insurance, or health industries may develop a set of Artifacts that are meaningful in their industries. The golden rule is that any new Artifact type must have a shape that does not conflict (or could easily be confused with) existing BPMN shapes.

It is possible that future versions of the BPMN specification will standardize further types of Artifacts.

Chapter 12.   Connectors

Connectors link two objects on a diagram. There are three differ-ent types of BPMN Connectors (see Figure 12-1):

- **Sequence Flow**—Defines the order of *flow object*s in a Process (Activities, Events, and Gateways).
- **Message Flow**—Defines the flow of communication be-tween two *participants* or *entities* (e.g., an organization and its suppliers). The object of the communication is a *mes-sage*.
- **Associations**—Used to link Artifacts (data and other in-formation) with other diagram objects, including *flow ob-jects* (Activities, Events, and Gateways).

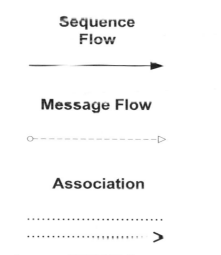

**Sequence
Flow**

Message Flow

Association

Figure 12-1—Three types of BPMN Connectors

Sequence Flow

Sequence Flow connects the other Process elements (Activities, Events, and Gateways). It orders the *flow objects*—for example, Activities such as "Send Invoice," "Receive Payment," and "Accept Payment" are performed sequentially in Figure 12-2. The Se-quence Flow of a Process—the solid lines with solid arrowheads in between the Activities in the figure—create the paths of the Proc-ess navigated during its performance.

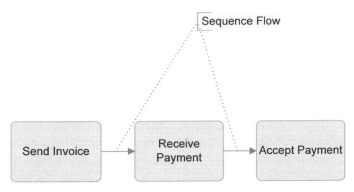

Figure 12-2—Sequence Flow within a Process

The source and target of the Sequence Flow line (the target shown by the arrowhead on the line) can only connect Events, Activities, and Gateways. Sequence Flow cannot connect any other BPMN elements, but most importantly, Sequence Flow <u>cannot</u> cross a Sub-Process boundary or Process boundary (a Pool).

Many modeling techniques and methodologies use the term "control flow" for the connectors between tasks and activities (similar to BPMN Sequence Flow). BPMN specifically does not use the term "control flow" for connectors. It was determined that there were many factors that "control" the performance of a Process or Activity and that the sequence of the activities was just one factor. Other factors that "control" Activities include: the arrival of *messages*, the availability of data, the availability of resources (such as performers), and built-in timing constraints (discussed in more detail in "Performing an Activity" on page 181).

Conditional Sequence Flow

A Sequence Flow has an internal attribute called *condition*.[36] However, the *condition* cannot be used in all circumstances. The *condition* attribute is <u>not available</u> when connecting from:

- An Event
- Event, Parallel, and Complex Gateways

The *condition* attribute is available when connecting from:

- Excusive and Inclusive Gateways
- Activities

---

[36] Attributes are generally not shown graphically. In this case, they do have a graphical representation (the condition is attached to the Sequence Flow).

The use and evaluation of the Sequence Flow *conditions* for Exclusive and Inclusive Gateways has been described above (see "Event Gateway Splitting Behavior" on page 136 and "Inclusive Gateway Splitting Behavior" on page 148).

When a *condition* is used on the *outgoing* Sequence Flow of an Activity, it is called A Conditional Sequence Flow. Since the *condition* controls the flow between Activities, a mini-diamond (like a mini-Gateway) appears at the beginning of the Connector (see Figure 12-3).

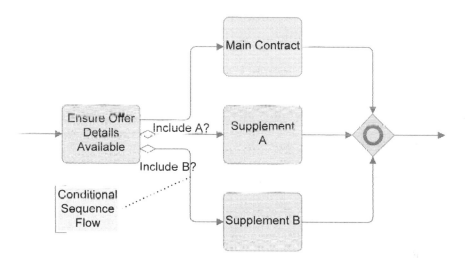

Figure 12-3—Conditional Sequence Flow may follow an Activity

When the Activity has completed and the *condition* evaluates to *true,* then a *token* (flow) will move down the Sequence Flow. If the *condition* evaluates to *false,* then the flow does not occur. The behavior of a set of Conditional Sequence Flow for an Activity is similar to that of an Inclusive Gateway (see "Inclusive Gateway Splitting Behavior" on page 148).

Such an Activity must have at least two *outgoing* Sequence Flow and at least one of the Sequence Flow must be guaranteed to occur (otherwise the Process might become stuck).

The modeler must always ensure that the combination of *conditions* represented in the *outgoing* Sequence Flow always leads to at least one of them firing for every performance of the Activity. One way to do that is to use a standard Sequence Flow or place a Default Sequence Flow on one of the Conditional Sequence Flow. Figure 12-3, above, uses a standard Sequence Flow following the "Ensure Offer Details Available" Task. Since there is no *condition* for that Sequence Flow, a *token* will move down that path. If a Default Sequence Flow is used (see the next section), a *token* will move down that path only when all the other *conditions* evaluate to *false*.

Best Practice: **Use a Standard or Default Sequence Flow when using Conditional Sequence Flow**—*One way for the modeler to ensure that the Process does not become stuck after an Activity is to use a standard or Default Sequence Flow whenever Conditional Sequence Flow are used (see Figure 12-3, above).*

Default Sequence Flow

In the last section, we discussed *conditions* used with some Sequence Flow. Alongside those *conditions* is a special BPMN *condition* called the *default condition*. The *default condition* can complement a set of standard *conditions* to provide an automatic escape mechanism in case all the standard *conditions* evaluate to *false*.

The Sequence Flow that has this *default condition* is called Default Sequence Flow. The Default Sequence Flow has a hatch mark near its beginning (see Figure 12-4).

In the example, on the *outgoing* Sequence Flow of the Exclusive Gateway, it is possible for all *conditions* to return *false*. In such circumstances, the Process will become stuck. The *default condition* gets around this problem.

The detail of the mechanism is as follows (to ensure that at least one *condition* of a set of *conditions* is *true*). If any of the set of standard *conditions* evaluates to *true*, then the *default condition* is *false*. If all of the standard *conditions* return *false*, then the *default condition* becomes *true*.

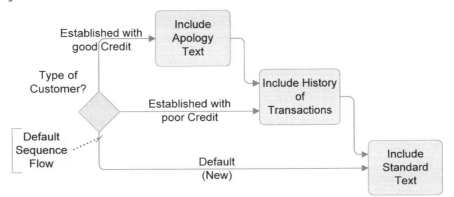

Figure 12-4—An example of Default Sequence Flow

The Default Sequence Flow can be used in all situations where a set of *outgoing* Sequence Flow can have *conditions*. In BPMN, these situations are:

- Exclusive Gateways
- Inclusive Gateways
- Activities

Message Flow

Message Flow defines the messages/communications between two separate *participants* (shown as Pools) of the diagram (see Figure 12-5). They are drawn with dashed lines that have a small hollow circle at the beginning and a hollow arrowhead at the end.

Message Flow must always occur between <u>two separate Pools</u> and <u>cannot</u> connect two objects within a single Pool. Thus, Message Flow is only used in collaborations (diagrams with two or more Pools).

As shown in Figure 12-5 below, Message Flow can connect to the boundary of the Pool (for a *black box* Pool). Alternatively, Message Flow can connect to a *flow object* within a Pool (if expanded with its own Process details).

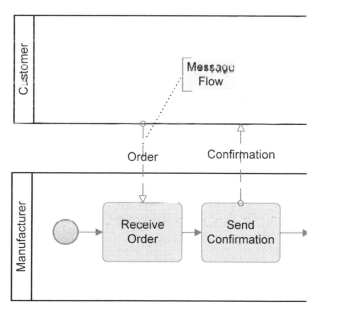

Figure 12-5—Message Flow between two Pools (*participants*)

Key Point: *There is a strong distinction between* Sequence Flow *and* Message Flow. Sequence Flow *can only be used within a Pool and* Message Flow *can only be used across Pools.*

Many modelers ask why Message Flow cannot be used within a Pool. Processes already have a mechanism to move data between Activities—*data flow* (see page 176). Therefore, there is no reason to use a *message* to send data from one part of a Process to another part of the same Process since the "process data" is made available everywhere to the entire process.[37] Furthermore, using Message Flow within a Process would corrupt the clean separation between Sequence Flow and Message Flow, and would create confusion for modelers trying to make decisions about Process structure (e.g., what data mechanism should they use).

If a *message* is truly required between two Activities, then this would indicate that the Activities reside in two separate contexts or loci of control. That is, the Activities should be modeled in two separate Pools.

Association

An Association will link one diagram object (i.e. creates a relationship) with another diagram object (such as Artifacts and Activities). For example, the dotted line that connects a Text Annotation to another object is actually an Association (see Figure 12-6).

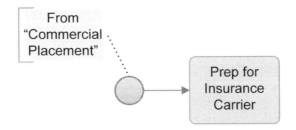

Figure 12-6—Associations connect Annotations to Objects

One of the more important uses of Associations is to show that data is input and output from Activities, e.g. an "Order" is output from one Activity and input into a later Activity (as in Figure 12-7). The directional line (with an open arrowhead) shows the source and target of the Data Object (a type of Artifact).

---

[37] BPMN does not specify how data flow should be implemented by a BPMS engine. Such transfers of data may, use an underlying messaging system. Other systems may use other mechanisms. But such details are transparent to the modeler and the Processes should behave the same way regardless of the underlying technology used.

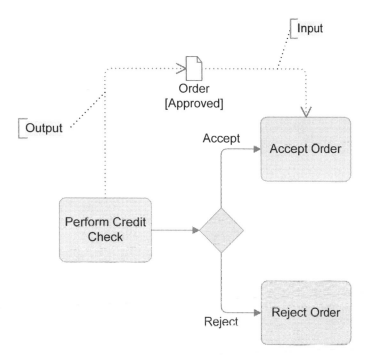

Figure 12-7—Associations used to show the flow of data

We discuss the flow of data into and out of Activities in more detail in "Data Flow" on page 176.

Normal Flow

The concept of *normal flow* is often referred to as the "Happy Path" or the "Skinny Process." [38] *Normal flow* refers to core Process, where the *flow objects* (Events, Activities, and Gateways) are connected through Sequence Flow, beginning with a Start Event and following the core alternative and parallel paths until the Process completes at an End Event (see Figure 12-8). *Normal flow* does not include Exception Flow or Compensation Flow.

---

[38] In reality, the Happy Path may actually be a sub-set of Normal Flow. For example, the high-probability conditions for decisions might make up the Happy Path, while other, less probable paths are part of the Normal Flow (but not happy).

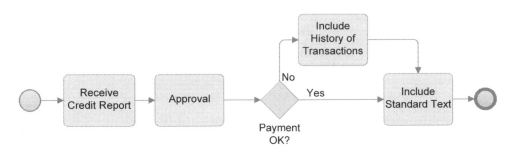

Figure 12-8—The *normal flow* of a Process

The *normal flow* describes the core structure of the Process. Focusing on the *normal flow* enables the modeler to create a relatively simple, flow-chart diagram. The additional features of BPMN (such as Artifacts, Swimlanes and Exception Flow) provide extra detail if needed.

One of the general rules for BPMN is that Sequence Flow must make it from the start to the finish without any "assumptions" (implicit areas where the Sequence Flow somehow magically jumps from one place to another). This is one of the reasons for the *default condition* at Exclusive Gateways to ensure that flow is explicitly shown.

Data Flow

Data flow represents the movement of Data Objects from into and out of Activities. With many process-modeling notations, the movement of data and the flow of Activities (control flow) are tightly coupled. However, in BPMN, *data flow* is decoupled from the Sequence Flow. Sequence Flow handles the ordering of the Activities. Directed Associations handle the flow of data to and from Activities. It is possible to combine the Sequence Flow and the *data flow* when they coincide, but they are natively separated to allow modeling flexibility.

In Figure 12-9, an Association exiting the first Task connects to the Data Object (the output) and an Association connected from the same Data Object is then input to the second Task.

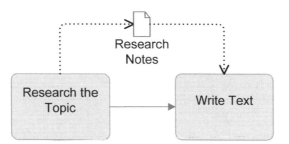

Figure 12-9—A Data Object as *output* and *input* to Activities

When there is a simple progression of *data flow* from one Activity to another, the *data flow* is more clearly defined (less clutter) by binding the Data Object to the Sequence Flow (see Figure 12-10). An Association connects the Data Object to the Sequence Flow between the two Activities. It means that the Artifact is the output of the first Task and the input to the second. Thus, the diagram in Figure 12-9 is equivalent to the diagram in Figure 12-10.

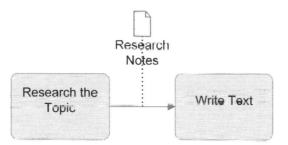

Figure 12-10—A Data Object bound to a Sequence Flow

While it is possible to associate a Data Object to a Sequence Flow that connects to a Gateway, we do not recommend this type of configuration. It can quickly become difficult to understand how the *inputs* and *outputs* are applied to the Activities on both sides of the Gateway. This is particularly true where a string of Gateways is used. In BPMN 1.1, this type of Association is not restricted. In BPMN 2.0, there will be a clarification (and probably some restrictions) placed on this type of model configuration.

Best Practice: **Do not Associate a Data Object with a Sequence Flow if the Sequence Flow is connected to a Gateway**—*The application of* inputs *and* outputs *are easily confused when one or more Gateways is used for Sequence Flow that are associated with Data Objects.*

The reason that BPMN decoupled the *data flow* from Sequence Flow is clear in Figure 12-11. The *output* of the "Receive Book Request" Task is not *input* into the next Task, it is input into an Activity that is further downstream in the Process (the "E-Mail Return Reminder" Task). Also, there is a Gateway in between the two activities. These kinds of situations make the tight coupling of data and Sequence Flow misleading and confusing. The Data Object would have to be dragged through all the intervening Activities and the Gateway, even though it would was not used or referenced.

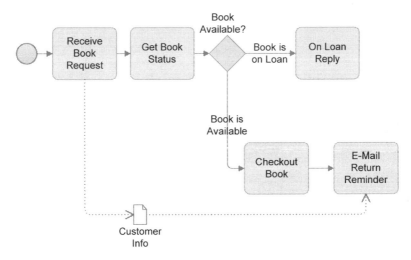

Figure 12-11—Decoupling Sequence Flow and *data flow*

As mentioned earlier, the Sequence Flow and the *flow objects* (Activities, Events, and Gateways) represent the underlying structure (*normal flow*) of a Business Process. Therefore, a tool might hide or display Data Objects (or all Artifacts and Associations) without changing the underlying structure of the Process.

More Complex Activity Inputs and Outputs

In complex Processes, the organization of *inputs* and *outputs* between Activities can also be complex. While not necessarily graphically obvious, BPMN provides the underlying mechanisms to handle this complexity.

"*Inputsets*" are used to group *incoming* Artifacts (*inputs*). All Activities have at least one *inputset*, but they are not apparent when there is only one *input*. If there is more than one *input*, they are grouped into one or more *inputsets*. However, in some cases a single *input* may be a part of more than one *inputset*.

The purpose for grouping *inputs* is to combine pieces of incomplete data into one complete set of data that is sufficient for the Activity to begin work.

Where there is more than one *inputset*, only one is required to in-stantiate the Activity. The first *inputset* that is complete will allow the start of the Activity. If more than one of the *inputsets* is com-plete, then the *inputset* that is first on the list of *inputsets* (for the Activity) will be used. Note that there are other factors that affect the start of an Activity, which will be described in "Performing an Activity" on page 181.

Figure 12-12 shows that the complete *input* to the "Review Report" Task is a Report, but depending on what happened prior to the Task, the Report may arrive as one document (one *input* in one *inputset*), or may arrive in two parts (two *inputs* in another *input-set*). Task performance will require either the full document or the two parts, but not a mixture. That is, if "Report Part 1" arrives, the Task cannot begin until "Report Part 2" arrives.[39] If the "Full Report" arrives at any time before the Task starts, then that *in-putset* would be satisfied and the Task can start.

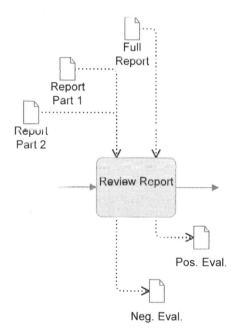

Figure 12-12—Multiple Activity Inputs and Outputs

There are no graphical markers or indicators to differentiate be-tween *inputsets*. They are considered part of the Activity details, which would add too much complexity to the diagram if exposed. However, there are ways to help the reader of the diagram to see

---

[39] Actually, there are more advanced attribute settings that would allow initiation with just one of the Parts.

where different *inputsets* are being used. The modeler can connect all Associations of an *inputset* to the same point on the Activity boundary. Figure 12-12 above shows how the two different *inputsets* for the Activity are connected to two separate points on the Activity boundary. On the other hand, where the Annotation arrows of the two *inputs* that make up a single *inputset* are combined, it is clear they make up the elements of that *inputset*. It is not required to connect the Associations in this way, but it is a convenient way to show that two (or more) Artifacts belong to the same *inputset*.[40]

Outputsets can also group *outgoing* Artifacts (*outputs*). For a single instantiation of an Activity, only one *outputset* is produced. The work of the Activity hides the decision as to which *outputset* is chosen. In this example (Figure 12-12 above), the evaluation will either be positive or negative (but not both).

As with the grouping of Associations connection points for *inputsets*, if an Activity produces two *outputs* that are part of the same *outputset*, a best practice is to show them coming out the same point on the Activity.

It is also possible to create a mapping from a specific *inputset* to a particular *outputset*—i.e. if *inputset* "One" arrives, then produce *outputset* "Two." The definition of the mapping between *inputsets* and *outputsets* is all done within the attributes of the Activity (none of these attributes are shown graphically).

Best Practice: ***Modeling** inputsets—If there is more than one* inputset, *pick a point on the boundary of an Activity and have all* inputs *that belong to a single* inputset *connect to that point. The* inputs *for the other* inputsets *should each connect to separate points on the boundary of the Activity. The same pattern should apply to modeling* outputsets.

---

[40] In our workshops, delegates have struggled to appreciate the reason for *inputsets*. They appear confusing since two different *inputs* (that are not modeled as an *inputset*) by default, they would both be required before the Activity *state* would change to *running* (see The Life-Cycle of an Activity on page 181 for Activity *states*). The reason for *inputsets* is only fully understood when delegates are asked to find a way of modeling that an Activity can start when either one set of *inputs,* or another, is available (as in Figure 12-12 above). This is a complex area, and in BPMN the decision was taken to provide the flexibility but without having an impact on the quality of the diagram. There is always a trade-off between the detail that is shown in the diagram vs. what is hidden in element attributes.

Chapter 13.   Advanced Concepts

Performing an Activity

A Process model can capture a lot of information about how work happens. The position of an Activity within the Process, and the related Activity information, will affect how and when it is performed.

The first constraint on the Activity is its position in the Process, relative to other Activities (defined by Sequence Flow). By definition, the performance cannot start until the *token* arrives on its *incoming* Sequence Flow. As shown in Figure 13-1, the "Send Rejection" Task must complete before the "Archive Details" Sub-Process can occur.

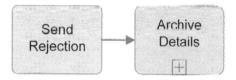

Figure 13-1—Sequence Flow is the main constraint on an Activity

We describe the other constraints on the performance of an Activity in the next section.

The Life-Cycle of an Activity

At the start of an Activity, (i.e. when a *token* arrives at the Activity), its *state* changes making it "*ready.*" This does not mean that the Activity immediately starts. It only means that the Process has reached a *state* where the Activity <u>could</u> start. Other factors may also affect its performance.

For example, in Figure 13-2, the "Review Current Designs" Task has two separate *inputs* (design documents). If the *inputs* are not available when the *token* arrives, then the Task cannot start.

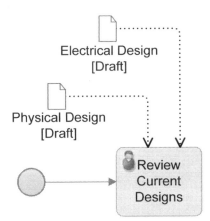

Figure 13-2—Multiple constraints on the performance of an Activity

Also, the icon of person in the above Task (and this is not part of the standard) might indicate that a person is involved. As with the inputs, if the person assigned to the Activity is not available, then the Activity cannot start. Note that it is not required to assign a specific person. A group of people or a business role could be assigned, but in the end, usually a single person will end up working on the Activity.

When all the constraints (e.g., *inputs*, etc.) are available, then Activity performance can begin—the Activity changes to a *state* of "*running.*" When the work of the Activity is finished, the Activity will change to a state of "*completed.*" While running, its *state* might change to "*paused,*" "*restarted*" or "*interrupted*" (through an Intermediate Event).

So a BPMN Activity goes through a series of *states* (its life-cycle) from the time that a *token* arrives until a *token* leaves the Activity. The types of states for an Activity include: *none, ready, active, cancelled, aborting, aborted, completing,* and *completed.* A single Activity *instance* will never go through all of these *states.* A typical cycle of *states* would be *none, ready, active, completing, completed,* and then back to *none.* However, an Activity can move into one or more of the other *states* under various circumstances, usually implying the triggering of an attached Intermediate Event.[41]

---

[41] A more detailed description of the Activity Life-Cycle is available on request from the authors.

Compensation and Transactions

In BPMN, a Transaction is a formal business relationship and agreement between two or more *participants*. For a Transaction to succeed, all parties involved have to perform their own Activities and reach the point where all parties are agreed. If any one of them withdraws or fails to complete, then the Transaction cancels and all parties then need to *undo* all the work that has completed.

A Process model (i.e., within one Pool), shows the Activities of the Transaction Sub-Process for just one of the *participants* (shown with a double line boundary—see Figure 13-3).

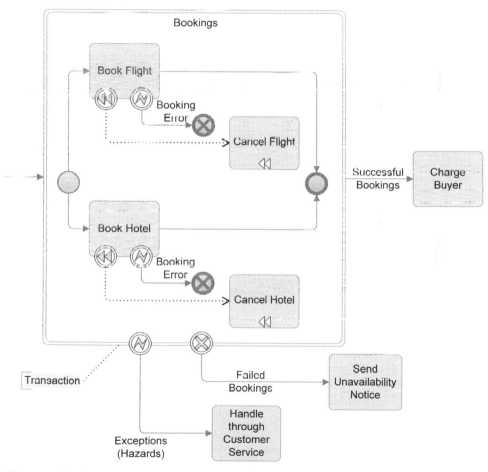

Figure 13-3—An example of a Transaction Sub-Process

Transaction Sub-Processes have special behaviors. Firstly, they are associated with a Transaction Protocol (e.g., WS-Transaction). This means that the companies involved in the Transaction must be able to send and receive all the hand-shaking *messages* between the *participants*. Most of these *messages* are not visible at the level of the Process, but are important to making sure that the Transaction progresses appropriately.

Secondly, if the work of all the Activities in the Transaction Sub-Process complete normally and all the *tokens* reach an End Event (see Figure 13-4), the Sub-Process is still not complete.

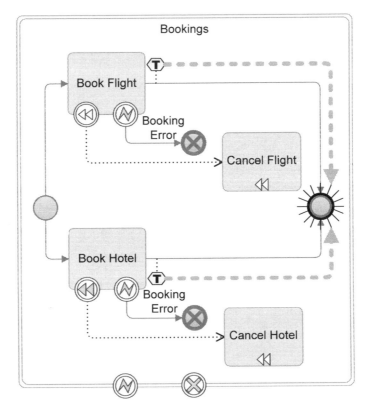

Figure 13-4—A Transaction Sub-Process is not quite done

Through the hand-shaking *messages*, there has to be unanimous agreement among the *participants* that everything is OK (i.e., that the other *participants'* Transactions also reached their end points successfully). Once that agreement occurs, the Transaction Sub-Process is complete and the *token* can continue in the *parent* Process (see Figure 13-5). Prior to this agreement, it would still be possible to cancel the whole Transaction Sub-Process if one of the parties cancelled.

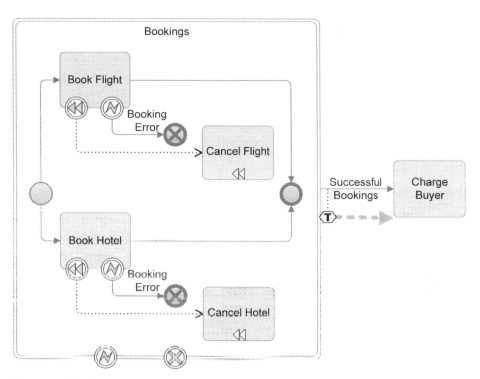

Figure 13-5—A Transaction Sub-Process is complete

Thirdly, if a processing or technical error occurs for one of the *participants* of the *transaction,* then there are two possibilities for interrupting the Transaction Sub-Process:

- An attached Error Intermediate Event is triggered (often called a *hazard*) and the Transaction Sub-Process is interrupted.

- An attached Cancel Intermediate Event and the Transaction Sub-Process is *cancelled.*

Hazards in a Transaction Sub-Process

When there is a *hazard*, the circumstances are so grievous that normal cancellation and *compensation* are not sufficient to fix the situation. The *transaction* is then interrupted in the same way that an Error Intermediate Event interrupts a normal Sub-Process (see section "Interrupting Activities with Events" on page 99). The error can happen within the Transaction Sub-Process or within a Process (unseen) of one the other *participants* in the *transaction*. The error from one of the other *participants* will be sent through the *transaction protocol*. The error generated by the Transaction Sub-Process is sent to the other *participants* through the *transaction protocol*.

When Error Intermediate Event attached to the boundary of the Transaction Sub-Process triggers, all work within the Sub-Process is terminated immediately—there is no *compensation*. The *token* then is sent down the *outgoing* Sequence Flow of the Error Event to reach Activities that will deal with the situation (see Figure 13-6).

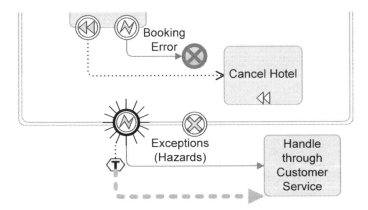

Figure 13-6—When a Transaction Sub-Process has a *hazard*

Cancellation in a Transaction Sub-Process

As with a Hazard, a Transaction Sub-Process can be cancelled through an Event internal to the Sub-Process or through a cancellation sent through a *transaction protocol*.

When a Transaction Sub-Process is *cancelled*, the Cancel Intermediate Event attached to its boundary is triggered (see Figure 13-7). The *token* will eventually continue down the Cancel Intermediate Event's *outgoing* Sequence Flow, but the behavior of the Transaction Sub-Process involves more than just interrupting the work in the Sub-Process.

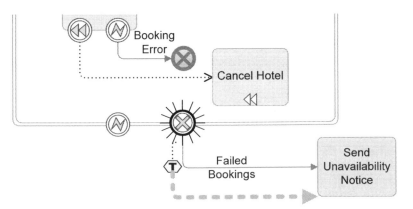

Figure 13-7—When a *Transaction* Sub-Process is Cancelled

Indeed, all ongoing work within the *transaction* is cancelled. However, completed work (in the Transaction Sub-Process) may need to be undone, which requires a "*rolling back*" before the *parent* Process can continue. This means that each Activity in turn, in reverse order, is checked to see whether or not it requires *compensation*. *Compensation* is the undoing of work that has been completed.

A *token* can be used to trace this *rolling back* as it travels backward through the Process (see Figure 13-8) after a Transaction Sub-Process has been cancelled. Many Activities, such as receiving a *message*, have nothing that requires undoing. But other Activities, such as those that update a database, require *compensation*. Each of these Activities will have a Compensation Intermediate Event attached to its boundary (the Event with a rewind symbol).

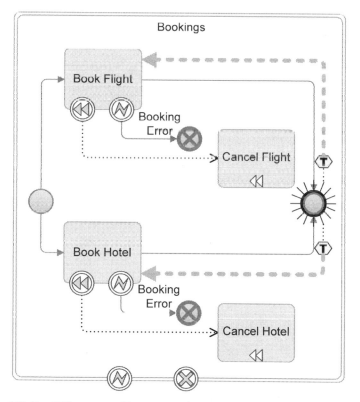

Figure 13-8—When a Transaction Sub-Process is *cancelled* the Sub-Process starts "*rolling back*"

Compensation does not just happen automatically. Another Activity is required to undo the work of the original Activity. A special Activity, a Compensation Activity (Activity shown with a rewind symbol) is used to undo the work. The Compensation Activity links to each Activity via the Compensation Intermediate Event attached to its boundary. The link between the normal Activity and the Compensation Activity is done through an Association rather than a Sequence Flow.

The Compensation Intermediate Event is never *triggered* during the normal flow of the Process. It only can be triggered during the *roll-back* of the Transaction Sub-Process. When the reversal of the *token* reaches an Activity that has an attached Compensation Intermediate Event <u>and</u> that Activity had completed normally (i.e., was not interrupted or incomplete), that Compensation Event fires (see Figure 13-9) and the *token* is then sent to the *associated* Compensation Activity.

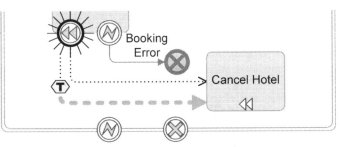

Figure 13-9—Compensation Intermediate Events are *triggered* to initiate Compensation Activities

The Compensation Activity has the "rewind" marker to distinguish it from Activities performed during the *normal flow—compensation* is never done during the normal activity of a Process. Since *compensation* is outside of *normal flow*, a *compensation* Association, instead of a Sequence Flow, links the Compensation Intermediate Event with the Compensation Activity (and through it, the Activity that needs to be *rolled back*). The Compensation Activity must not have any *incoming* or *outgoing* Sequence Flow. Only <u>one</u> Compensation Activity can be *associated* with the Compensation Intermediate Event. Tasks can be used, but often Sub-Processes are used since the work necessary to compensate is usually complex.

More precisely, an attached Compensation Intermediate Event only triggers if the Activity has completed normally and is in the *completed* state (see section "The Life-Cycle of an Activity" on page 181 for more information about Activity *states*). If the Activity is not yet completed, or was interrupted, then *Compensation* will not take place for that Activity.

When the Compensation Activity has completed, the *token* continues its backward journey through the *Transaction* by leaving the Activity whose work was just undone (see Figure 13-10).

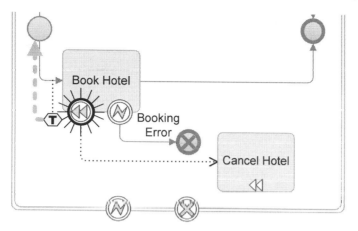

Figure 13-10—The *Transaction* completes the *roll-back*

When all the Activities of the Transaction Sub-Process have been checked and, if necessary, *compensated*, then the *cancellation* of the *Transaction* is completed. This allows the *token* in the *parent* Process to travel down the *outgoing* Sequence Flow of the attached Compensation Intermediate Event (see Figure 13-11).

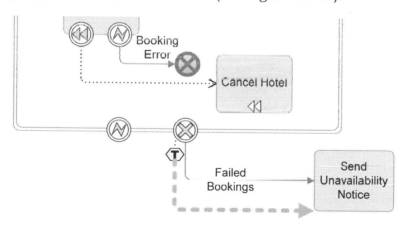

Figure 13-11—The Process continues after the *transaction* is *cancelled*

Compensation without a Transaction Sub-Process

An attached Compensation Intermediate Event (to an Activity) can also be *triggered* in any normal Process (not a *transaction*) when a downstream Compensation Intermediate Event or Compensation End Event "throws" the appropriate *trigger*. The *trigger* will either be the name of the Activity to be compensated or a global *compensation trigger*, which will fire all attached Compensation Intermediate Events.

Ad Hoc Processes

The Ad Hoc Process represents Processes where the Activities might occur in any order, and in any frequency—there is no specific ordering or obvious decisions. As such, an Ad Hoc Process represents another special type of BPMN Process. It has a marker, a Tilde (~), to show that it is Ad Hoc (see Figure 13-12). Typically, the Activities in an Ad Hoc Process involve *human performers* who make the decisions as to what Activities to perform, when to perform them, and how many times. For example, a software developer may need to write, test, and debug the code in any order and at any time.

Figure 13-12 presents a Process of developing a book chapter where it is necessary to research the topic, write the text, and add graphics, etc., yet it is impossible to specify and order or frequency in advance.

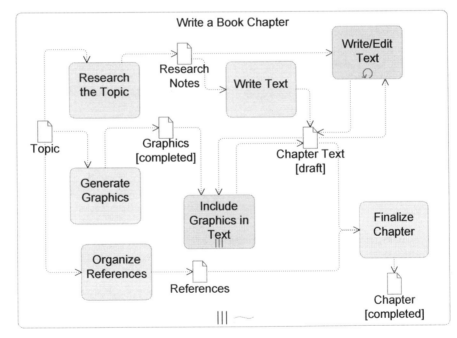

Figure 13-12—An Example of an Ad-Hoc Process

Although there is usually no Sequence Flow used within an Ad Hoc Process, it is possible to use occasional Sequence Flow between some of the Activities to show an ordered dependency between them. But the use of Sequence Flow does not imply that there is a specific start or a specific end to the Process.

It is also possible to show data *inputs* and *outputs* of the Activities.

As mentioned above, the *performer(s)* can undertake the Activities in any order and any number of times. Eventually the work of the Process is finished, but since there is no End Event to mark the end of Process, another mechanism is used. The Ad Hoc Process has a non-graphical *completion condition* attribute that is used to determine if the work of the Process is complete. At the start of the Process the attribute is *false*. When the attribute becomes *true*, the Process ends. The attribute only becomes *true* when the data expressed in the *condition* test is updated during the completion of one of the Ad Hoc Process's Activities.

Appendices

Process Execution Environments

Abstract: *This appendix is designed to give the reader a brief overview of the components of a modern BPM Suite.42*

The overall approach is not especially new—workflow systems have been around since the late 80s—but they are becoming more mature. XML and Web Services have solved many of the integration problems that plagued the approach through the 90s. Tools now include sophisticated monitoring environments, business rules integration, simulation mechanisms and facilities to manage the deployment of process models and other artifacts necessary for proper operation. As they have evolved, many vendors have adopted the term "BPM Suite" to describe the broad nature of their offering (see Figure 13 13).

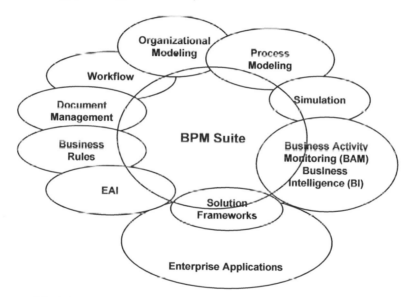

Figure 13-13—A Process Modeling component is an important element in a BPM Suite

Products often include capabilities to chain processes together or to bind fragments of process together at run time (based on the context of the case of work in hand).

---

42 For a more comprehensive discussion of BPM Suites and their capabilities, refer to "Mastering BPM – The Practitioners Guide" by Derek Miers.

In parallel with the functional evolution that has led to the emergence of the BPM Suite, the use of process models has also evolved. In the early days, they acted as a guide to developers who then configured the environment. Then vendors started to incorporate modeling capabilities into their products. Over time, these modeling environments became easier to use, but their capabilities were still constrained by the core capabilities of the underlying process engine—i.e., vendors only supported functionality that their proprietary engine needed.

With the appearance of block structured XML-based process languages such as BPML (Business Process Modeling Language) and later BPEL (Business Process Execution Language), the engine at the heart of the BPM Suite has now evolved to the point it can directly execute a process model (without translation to some proprietary intermediate form).

Techniques for Process Architecture

Abstract: *Our intention with this section is not imply a specific methodology; it is to highlight the issues and challenges, discussing some of the approaches available. We also point to a few key techniques that can assist on the journey toward process excellence.*

Functional Decomposition

Most of us immediately resort to Functional Decomposition[43] [44] — using it to break up the domain hierarchically, with one part contained within another.[45] This often causes problems—that hierarchical structure implies that the world is also hierarchically structured. Yet in reality, the modeler is <u>imposing</u> that structure as a way of simplifying the problem domain.

For example, the Customer Relationship Management (CRM) Process is not contained with Sales, or Marketing, or any other functional group for that matter; it is a "Capability" that the entire organization needs exhibit.

Moreover, Functional Decomposition tends to reinforce the very same silos that a process-oriented initiative is trying to break down. While it might be appealing to the software engineer as a way of breaking up a problem with a set of inputs and outputs to each step, the analogy starts to break down in the world of white-collar office work, services and customer relationships.

Key Point: *It is better to think of Processes as a network rather than some statically defined hierarchy.[46]*

Key Point: *As a general approach, Functional decomposition should be avoided.*

---

[43] Functional decomposition is a method of hierarchically structuring business functions, processes, and sub-processes within an organization. The British Cyberneticist Stafford Beer once aptly described Functional Decomposition as "a mechanism for apportioning blame".." Beer was responsible for the Viable System Model.

[44] Our use of Initial Capitals in this chapter is to provide emphasis for the key concepts discussed. Terms like Capabilities, Services and Functional Decomposition are <u>not</u> parts of the BPMN specification (elsewhere in the book we reserve the use of Initial Capitals to the graphical elements of BPMN).

[45] In BPMN, the Embedded Sub-Process concept supports functional decomposition. See Embedded Sub-Processes on page 70.

[46] Indeed, it is more accurate to think of them as a dynamic *network of interacting* process *instances.*

Process Composition

Another way of approaching the chunking problem is to compose Processes from a set of constituent parts. On the surface, this seems only subtly different from Functional Decomposition, but is dramatically different in terms of the flexibility and agility delivered.

Where Processes are composed of other Processes, the lower level Processes are also <u>reusable</u> in other processes (rather than constrained to a single context). Of course, this means that such processes require careful design and construction in order to support that reusable context. In a sense, each lower level Process provides a "Service" to a *parent* level Process.[47]

Business Services Oriented Architecture

While Process composition provides the mechanism, it still does not necessarily help the modeler decide on what processes are required.

Firstly, at the highest level, it is necessary to decide what the business is really all about. What Capabilities are required on an ongoing basis? Processes become ways of implementing those Capabilities through Services. At this level, we are discussing "Process as Purpose" rather than Process as a set of sequential Tasks or Activities.[48]

The trick is to think of the *outcomes* that are important to customers and other stakeholders, and then imagine the "Services" that will deliver those Capabilities. They should be the Services that will delight the customer and provide a superior customer experience. These Services will be composed of other Services, but eventually, a Process (procedure) implements a Service.

As a result, a set of Services implements a business level Capability is implemented through that are composed of other Services.[49]

The idea is that by understanding what capabilities and behaviors are required, it becomes possible to derive an appropriate set of

---

[47] In BPMN, the Reusable Sub-Process construction supports Process Composition (see Reusable Sub-Processes on page 71).

[48] For a more extensive discussion on these sorts of issues, see *Mastering Business Process Management—The Practitioner's Guide* by Derek Miers (published September 2008).

[49] We use a set of workshop techniques to support this quest, but they are outside the scope of this book. Those techniques draw on the Services DNA approach developed by Dr Allan Webster and others.

Processes and an organization that will support them. This is in stark contrast to the use of Functional Decomposition, where the existing organizational structure is usually the starting point.

Key Point: *Developing a high-level perspective on the Business Capabilities required for organizational success provides a context and scope to Process modeling work.*

Key Point: *A Business Services approach will allow the organization to align its Processes with the needs of customers and other stakeholders.*

From Business Context to Process Architecture

Having identified an appropriate business level scope, deriving the discrete Process Architecture is still a challenge. The best technique that we have come across for this is the Unit of Work (UoW) analysis.[50]

A UoW analysis involves bringing the relevant business people together in a workshop setting and brainstorming a long list of the Essential Business Entities (EBEs). Derived from an understanding what business the organization is, EBEs refer to the things that represent the "essence" or "subject matter" of the domain in question.

This list is then filtered to identify those items that have a "lifecycle" that the organization needs to manage. These are the Units of Work. For example, in a manufacturing organization, products are developed, taken to market, withdrawn, etc. For a standards body such as the OMG, "Specifications" are drafted, reviewed, approved, distributed, changed, withdrawn, etc.

Then it is a question of looking for the interactions between the Units of Work (Generates, Needs, Requires, Activates, Calls For, etc). One is trying to identify the dynamic relationships between these objects. Then, for each UoW, there will be three processes— Handle an Instance of, Manage the Flow of Instances and a Strategy Process that looks at improving the first two.

The net result is that, using the Unit of Work Analysis technique, it becomes possible to mechanically generate a Process Architec-

---

[50] Proposed by Martyn Ould in Chapter 6 of his book *Business Process Management—A Rigorous Approach*. This book is also the key reference for Role Activity Diagrams (RADs). RADs provide a powerful alternative representation of Process, combining both choreography (role interaction) with activities and instantiation.

ture for a given target domain.[51] This Process Architecture is based on the real world needs of that business having been validated and in a sense "designed" by the business specialists concerned.

Moreover, given access to the relevant subject matter experts, it is possible to complete the entire exercise in an afternoon. So regardless of the existing base, it is a valuable validation.

Further Reading

In large organizations, it becomes inordinately difficult to keep track of all the related artifacts and information on models, goals, objectives, and perspectives associated with the voyage toward process improvement and operational innovation.

The journey itself is an exercise in growing the organizational competence around business process. Within the OMG there are two specifications that help map out the route and allow an organization to manage the traceability of its assets in this area.[52]

- The Business Process Maturity Model (BPMM) might be thought of as describing the *journey* that an organization embarks upon when engaging in a business process driven transformation initiative. It describes the five stages of organizational maturity (in relation to business process) and the behaviors of an organization at that level of maturity.[53]
- The Business Motivation Model provides a scheme or structure for developing, communicating and managing business plans in an organized manner. Specifically, the Business Motivation Model identifies factors that motivate the creation of business plans, defining the elements of these business plans; and how all these factors and elements interrelate. Among these elements are those that provide governance for and guidance to the business— Business Policies and Business Rules.

---

[51] Again, this technique is outside the scope of this book. We introduce it here as it offers a viable method of deriving an appropriate Process Architecture—one that is not predicated on the reporting structure of the organization.

[52] In the final analysis, Business Process models are just one of the types of assets an organisation will need.

[53] BPMM is a fully developed maturity model that rigorously follows the principles of established SEI process maturity frameworks, e.g. CMMI. BPMM is oriented around the needs of the broader business community rather than the IT project orientation of CMMI and CMM. The BPMM incorporates improvements in coverage, structure, and interpretation developed since the publication of its predecessor maturity models.

BPMN Issues and Directions

Choreography versus Orchestration

As its core, BPMN is fundamentally a flow diagram oriented notation—i.e., it focuses upon the "orchestration" of a Process. More specifically, it views Processes as a sequence of steps viewed from the perspective of the organization that needs to carry out the work.

BPMN can represent a simple chorcography-oriented view[54] using Message Flow between Pools. But it is difficult to represent the "derived process" that exists in between these Pools. Providing a comprehensive mechanism for modeling *choreographies* is a requirement for the development of BPMN 2.0

Collaborative Decisions and Meetings

As the flow diagram paradigm is applied, work assignment is usually represented via grouping of Activities within Lanes (usually representing organizational roles). As a result, it becomes very difficult (if not impossible) to reliably represent a collaborative decision (where several organizational roles interact to make a decision).

BPMN Futures

With the release of BPMN 2.0, the specification is going to change dramatically. However, the look-and-feel of the notation will remain the same—i.e., a BPMN 2.0 diagram will look much the same as a BPMN 1.1 diagram.

While the acronym (BPMN) remains the same, the words change subtly—it will become Business Process Model and Notation (instead of Modeling Notation). While this change appears trivial, the emphasis is now on a notation linked to an explicit meta-model and serialization format (storage mechanism). The inclusion of a storage format and metamodel will enable model portability between different vendors tools, yet still provide adequate facilities for vendors to extend and differentiate their products.

Graphically, we will see the inclusion of features to better support *choreography*—there will be a new *choreography* diagram defined in the specification. A *choreography* diagram will either standalone, or it could appear within the context of a broader *collaboration* diagrams (diagrams that include Pools).

---

[54] The interactions of the participants involved

Some of the new features expected in BPMN 2.0:

- A choreography diagram.
- A conversation diagram (related to choreography and collaboration).
- A new type of Intermediate Event: Escalation, which is like a type of error (and has the same scope) except that it does not interrupt Activities.
- An option on attached Intermediate Events such that they do not interrupt. This will support *triggers* such as Timer, Message, Escalation, Signal, Conditional, and Multiple.
- Specialized Event Sub-Processes—a type of optional Sub-Process used for non-interrupting Activities or compensation. This will support *Triggers* such as Timer, Message, Escalation, Signal, Conditional, Compensation, and Multiple.
- An extension to the definition of human activities.
- Formalization or enhancement of various technical infrastructures; such as execution semantics, mapping to BPEL, Event composition and correlation, use of services, and extension mechanisms.
- An XML schema exchange format for portability (also a XMI version for UML tools). The exchange will work for both model (semantic) information and for diagram layout.

Subsequent versions (following the BPMN 2.0 release) will likely include a number of "compliance levels" (so that vendors can explicitly state the degree of direct BPMN support they provide). This contrasts with the current situation where a vendor can claim BPMN support with just a few of the shapes represented graphically, ignoring the rest of the specification. Indeed, a quick survey of BPMN tool support reveals significant degrees of variability in terms of the support provided.

We expect to see the BPMN 2.0 pass through the relevant committees at the OMG by the end of Q1 2009. It is unlikely to emerge before the end of Q2 2009 (and that will be in Beta form).

BPMN Best Practices

This appendix collates the individual *best practices* identified throughout the book:

Best Practice: **Sending and Receiving Messages**—*The modeler could choose to use only Send and Receive Tasks, or to use only the throw and catch Message Intermediate Events. The Best Practice is to avoid mixing both approaches together in the same model.*

                  There are advantages and disadvantages to both approaches. Message Intermediate Events give the same result and have the advantage of being graphically distinguishable (whereas the Tasks are not). On the other hand, using Tasks, rather than the Events can enable the modeler to assign resources and simulate costs.

Best Practice: **Use of Start Events**—*In general, we recommend that modelers use Start and End Events.*

Best Practice: **Setting Timers**—*avoid specific date and time conditions as they inhibit the re-usability of the process.*

Best Practice: **Use a Default Condition**   *One way for the modeler to ensure that the Process does not get stuck at an Exclusive Gateway is to use a default condition for one of the outgoing Sequence Flow. This creates a Default Sequence Flow (see "Default Sequence Flow" on page 172). The Default is chosen if <u>all</u> the other Sequence Flow conditions turn out to be false.*

Best Practice: **Use a Timer Intermediate Event with an Event Gateway**—*One way for the modeler to ensure that the Process does not get stuck at an Event Based Exclusive Gateway is to use a Timer Intermediate Event as one of the options for the Gateway.*

Best Practice: **Ensure that the number of incoming Sequence Flow is correct for a Parallel Gateway**—*The key point is to exercise care, ensuring that merging Parallel Gateways have the correct number of incoming Sequence Flow—especially when used in conjunction with other Gateways. As a guide, modelers should match merging and splitting Parallel Gateways (if the desired behavior is to merge them again).*

Best Practice: **Use a Default Condition on an Inclusive Gateway**—*One way for the modeler to ensure that the Process does not get stuck at an Inclusive Gateway is to use a default condition for one of* the outgoing Sequence Flow. This Default Sequence Flow will always evaluate to true *if all the other Sequence Flow conditions turn out to be* false *(see "Default Sequence Flow" on page 172).*

Best Practice: **Always use Inclusive Gateways in pairs**—*A way to avoid unexpected behavior is to create models where a* merging *Inclusive Gateway follows a* splitting *Inclusive Gateway and that the number of Sequence Flow match between them.*

Best Practice: **Use a Text Annotation with the Complex Gateway**—*Since the actual behavior of a Complex Gateway will vary for each usage of the Gateway, use a Text Annotation to tell the reader of the diagram what behavior the Gateway is set to perform (see Figure 9-32).*

Best Practice: **Use a Standard or Default Sequence Flow when using Conditional Sequence Flow**—*One way for the modeler to ensure that the Process does not become stuck after an Activity is to use a standard or Default Sequence Flow whenever Conditional Sequence Flow are used.*

Best Practice: **Do not Associate a Data Object with a Sequence Flow if the Sequence Flow is connected to a Gateway**—*The application of inputs and outputs can be easily confused when one or more Gateways is used for Sequence Flow that are associated with Data Objects.*

Best Practice: **Modeling Inputsets**—*If there is more than one inputset, pick a point on the boundary of an Activity and have all inputs that belong to a single inputset connect to that point. The inputs for the other inputsets should each connect to separate points on the boundary of the Activity. The same pattern should apply to modeling outputsets.*

Afterword

If you wanted to make a cup of coffee, would you draw a diagram to describe the process? Probably not. The process is simple, we can easily memorize the necessary steps, and we typically perform all of the process steps by ourselves. Michael Hammer famously said, "If it doesn't make three people angry it isn't a process."[55] But if you wanted to teach somebody how to make coffee, or if you wanted to build an automated espresso machine, or if you wanted to standardize how hundreds of franchises of your coffee empire operate, the utility of visual process diagrams becomes immediately apparent.

Natural language is fraught with ambiguity—we often need to understand the context of a particular sentence in order to make sense of it. Process modeling languages reduce this ambiguity by limiting the amount of symbols (i.e. words) we can use to construct diagrams (i.e. sentences). Moreover, every element of a modeling language typically has a well-defined meaning, which reduces the amount of interpretation needed to understand a diagram.

When diagramming processes it is important to select a perspective that is appropriate to analyze the problem at hand, and the choice of perspective has implications on the choice of technique. The analysis of processes can focus on three possible perspectives: Activities, Resources, or Objects.

Object-centric process analysis places at the center the subject that is being processed. In the case of a procurement process, the purchase order itself would be the focal object, and the possible process paths are defined by the state changes that the purchase order can go through. Object-centric analysis is useful in processes where the central object is a document or a physical artifact that shapes the process and the resources needed to move it towards a desired target state.

Resource-centric process analysis places the emphasis on the participants that carry out actions in the process. In this world view the processing object is passed between workstations that each have capabilities and perform actions on the object that are appropriate given the characteristics of the object. This view is particularly appropriate if a process takes place within a fixed infrastructure that is too costly or risky to adapt. Resource-based

---

[55] Hammer, M. (1996): Beyond Reengineering. Harper Collins.

analysis may uncover social network structures that point to necessary changes in the organizational chart.

Activity-centric process analysis focuses on the processing tasks themselves, their sequencing, and the conditions for their activation and completion. This is the area addressed by the majority of process modeling languages.

The Business Process Modeling Notation (BPMN) is not without precedent—standard diagramming techniques for processes have been developed as early as the 1920s. Flowcharts for administrative procedures and Nassi-Schneiderman diagrams for structured programming were among the first widely used techniques. Project management brought us Gantt Charts and PERT network diagrams. Carl Adam Petri's dissertation on Communicating with Automata led to Petri Nets, which have in turn been refined into colored, hierarchical, workflow, and other kinds of net diagrams. The object-oriented development methodologies of the 1980s gave way to the Unified Modeling Language, which brought Sequence Diagrams and Activity Diagrams to describe the behavior of a system. So why did the world need another process modeling language?

For one, BPMN integrates capabilities from a number of its predecessors. It combines organizational swimlanes from Activity Diagrams with messaging concepts from Sequence Diagrams, introduces a large selection of event types and multiple ways to hierarchically decompose complex processes. The combination of language elements makes it a highly expressive language.[56] This expressiveness has a price, though. With more than 50 graphical symbols there often are multiple ways to capture the same process content.[57]

There are three aspects to the richness of BPMN: What the language is capable of expressing, what modelers currently use it for, and what modelers should use it for. BPMN is a rich notation, but

[56] Rosemann, Michael; Recker, Jan; Indulska, Marta and Peter Green: A Study of the Evolution of the Representational Capabilities of Process Modeling Grammars, in E. Dubois and K. Pohl, eds., Advanced Information Systems Engineering - CAiSE 2006, Vol. 4001, Lecture Notes in Computer Science, Luxembourg, Grand-Duchy of Luxembourg: Springer, 2006, pp. 447-461.

[57] zur Muehlen, Michael; Recker, Jan; Indulska, Marta: Sometimes Less is More: Are Process Modeling Languages Overly Complex? In: Taveter, K.; Gasevic, D. (Eds.): The 3rd International Workshop on Vocabularies, Ontologies and Rules for The Enterprise (VORTE 2007). Baltimore, MD, October 15th, 2007, IEEE Publishers.

knowing all the symbols does not guarantee that a modeler will create sensible diagrams, just like learning all words of the English language does not automatically turn us into a new Ernest Hemingway. In fact, in a recent survey of 120+ BPMN diagrams we have found plenty of modeling errors, and in some instances these errors were deliberate attempts to point out weaknesses in as-is models.[58]

Here is an example from a large government agency process in BPMN 1.0 format:

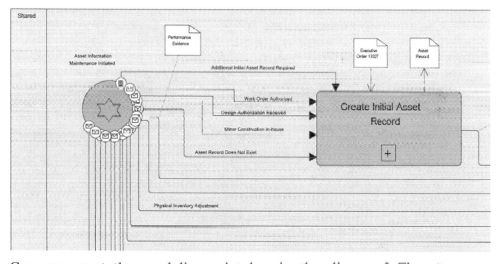

Can you spot the modeling mistakes in the diagram? There are two: An event cannot have any attached events, and the start event symbol cannot be attached to any other symbol. Mistakes like these are easily remedied with some training. The overall style of this example leads to a more important question: What was the intention of the modeler, and how could this intention be expressed in a correct, concise, and comprehensible way? In the example above the modeler was confronted by a process that can be triggered by a number of incoming documents that may arrive in a variety of combinations. The modeler chose to capture every possible incoming message in detail while the first process activity is at a comparatively high level. This mismatch of levels of abstraction is not cured by an intense study of the BPMN standard alone. The standard just spells out what constitutes a correct dia-

---

[58] zur Muehlen, Michael; Recker, Jan: How Much Language is Enough? Theoretical and Practical Use of the Business Process Modeling Notation, 20th International Conference on Advanced Information Systems Engineering (CAiSE 2008), Montpellier, France, June 16-20, 2008, Springer LNCS, pp. 465-479.

gram, not what constitutes a good diagram. Drawing good diagrams requires the aid of a style guide, just as an aspiring author complements an English dictionary with a guidebook such as the Elements of Style.

Since its inception, BPMN has been eagerly adopted by both practitioners and academics, and is being taught in training seminars and university classes around the world. Tool support is building, and a growing number of organizations have declared BPMN the corporate standard for process modeling. But much remains to be done.

Aspiring modelers and seasoned practitioners alike need authoritative guidance in terms of how BPMN can be used to maximum effect. The book in your hands, written by two experts on the subject matter, provides this guidance in a comprehensive and clearly structured fashion. It provides advice that affects both the substance and the style of your process diagrams.

It is my hope that the lessons in this book will help you improve the quality of your process designs. Better process designs improve communication, and this will in turn lead to better business results. So let's turn the page on bad process models.

Michael zur Muehlen,

Stevens Institute of Technology, USA

Author Biographies

Stephen A. White, Ph.D.

Email: wstephe@us.ibm.com
BPM Architect
IBM Corp.

Stephen A. White is currently a BPM Architect at IBM. He has 25 years experience with process modeling—ranging from developing models, consulting, training, process modeling tool design, product management, and standards development. In the mid-1990s he was product manager at Holosofx (which was later acquired by IBM), where he gained a lot of experience with the business analyst's perspective through training and consulting. After Holosofx, he was at SeeBeyond (later acquired by Sun Microsystems) where he began working in standards, including the start of BPMN. From SeeBeyond he moved to IBM where he continued work in standards and with BPMN.

While at SeeBeyond and IBM, he served on the BPMI.org Board of Directors (which later merged with the OMG). Within the OMG, he is currently a member of the BPM Steering Committee and is co-chair of an Architecture Board sponsored Special Interest Group on Process Metamodels.

As Working Group chair and Specification Editor since its inception, Stephen A. White was instrumental in creating the BPMN standard and is now guiding its continuing refinement at the OMG.

Derek Miers

Email: miers@bpmfocus.org
Industry Analyst and Technology Strategist
BPM Focus

Derek Miers is a well-known independent industry analyst and technology strategist. He delivers world-class training and consulting around BPMN, Process Architecture and BPM in general.

Over the years, he has carried out a wide range of consulting roles including running hundreds of training courses (in business and process modeling techniques), undertaking detailed technology selection assessments and project-risk assessment studies. Other engagements have involved the provision of strategic consulting advice from facilitating board level conversations around BPM initiatives, through establishing effective BPM Project and Expertise

Centers, to helping clients develop new business models that leverage business process strategies.

Clients have included many of the world's largest and well-known financial services companies (banks, building societies and insurers), pharmaceutical companies, telecoms providers, commercial businesses, product vendors and governmental organizations.

As Co-Chairman of BPMI.org, he helped merge the organization with the OMG and sits on the BPM Steering Committee of the OMG. At BPMI.org he helped create the BPM Think Tank event, and within the OMG, he continues to play an active role in its organization and delivery. He continues to play an active role in the creation of process related standards.

Derek Miers is also author of *Mastering BPM—A Practitioners Guide*, published by MK Press (ISBN 0-929652-46-0).

Foreword

Richard Mark Soley, Ph.D.

Email: soley@omg.org
Chairman and Chief Executive Officer
Object Management Group, Inc. (OMG®)

Dr. Richard Mark Soley is Chairman and Chief Executive Officer of the Object Management Group, Inc. (OMG®) and Executive Director of the SOA Consortium.

As Chairman and CEO of the OMG, Dr. Soley is responsible for the vision and direction of the world's largest consortium of its type. Dr. Soley joined the nascent OMG as Technical Director in 1989, leading the development of OMG's world-leading standardization process and the original CORBA® specification. In 1996, he led the effort to move into vertical market standards (starting with healthcare, finance, telecommunications and manufacturing) and modeling, leading first to the Unified Modeling Language (UML®) and later the Model Driven Architecture (MDA®). He also led the effort to establish the SOA Consortium in January 2007.

Previously, Dr. Soley was a cofounder and former Chairman/CEO of A. I. Architects, Inc., maker of the 386 HummingBoard and other PC and workstation hardware and software. Prior to that, he consulted for various technology companies and venture firms on matters pertaining to software investment opportunities. Dr. Soley has also consulted for IBM, Motorola, PictureTel, Texas Instruments, Gold Hill Computer and others. He began his professional life at Honeywell Computer Systems working on the Multics operating system.

A native of Baltimore, Maryland, U.S.A., Dr. Soley holds the bachelor's, master's and doctoral degrees in Computer Science and Engineering from the Massachusetts Institute of Technology.

Angel Luis Diaz, Ph.D.

Email: aldiaz@us.ibm.com
Director, Websphere Business Process Management
IBM Software Group

Dr. Angel Luis Diaz is IBM's Director for Websphere Business Process Management development, architecture and technology strategy.

Prior to this role, Dr. Diaz was responsible for IBM Software Group Technology Strategy and SOA Innovation. His team was responsible for driving the support of Web services technology across IBM's entire product line and combined offerings.

Before joining the IBM Software Group in 2003, Dr. Diaz was a member of IBM's Research staff and Senior Manager, where he led advanced technology projects related to XML & Web Services. In 2002, Dr. Diaz initiated the world's first two standards that make use of web services, the Organization for the Advancement of Structured Information Standards (OASIS) Web Services For Remote Portals (WSRP) and OASIS Web Services For Interactive Applications (WSIA). As a result, Dr. Diaz was nominated to the OASIS Technical Advisory Board, a body that defined the technical agenda for future OASIS standards work. In 1998 Dr. Diaz was co-chair and co-author of the first XML standard, the World Wide Web Consortium (W3C) Mathematical Markup Language (MathML). Since then, Dr. Diaz served on seven W3C activities including the Extensible Style Language (XSL), Cascading Style Sheets (CSS) and Document Object Model (DOM).

Dr. Diaz received his Ph.D. in computer science (distributed computing, programming languages & computer algebra) from Rensselaer Polytechnic Institute.

Afterword

Michael zur Muehlen Ph.D.

Email: mzurmuehlen@stevens.edu
Director, Center of Excellence in Business Process Innovation

Howe School of Technology Management
Stevens Institute of Technology, United States

Dr. Michael zur Muehlen is Assistant Professor of Information Systems at Stevens Institute of Technology in Hoboken, NJ. He directs Stevens' BPM research center (Center of Excellence in Business Process Innovation) and is responsible for the University's graduate program in Business Process Management and Service Innovation. Prior to his appointment at Stevens, Michael was a senior lecturer at the Department of Information Systems, University of Muenster, Germany, and a visiting lecturer at the University of Tartu, Estonia. He has over 14 years of experience in the field of process automation and workflow management, and has led numerous process improvement and design projects in Germany and the US and serves as Enterprise Chief Process Architect of the U.S. Department of Defense Business Transformation Agency. An active contributor to standards in the BPM area, Michael was named a fellow of the Workflow Management Coalition in 2004 and chairs the WfMC working group "Management and Audit." He studies the practical use of process modeling standards, techniques to manage operational risks in business processes, and the integration of business processes and business rules. SAP Research, the US Army, the Australian Research Council, and private sponsors have funded his research. Michael has presented his research in more than 20 countries. He is the author of a book on workflow-based process controlling, numerous journal articles, conference papers, book chapters and working papers on process management and workflow automation. He has also published widely on BPM standards and standard making in general. He is a founding director of the AIS special interest group on process automation and management (SIGPAM) . Michael holds a PhD (Dr. rer. pol.) and an MS in Information Systems from the University of Muenster, Germany.

Glossary

Activity:

An Activity represents the work performed within a business process. It has a rounded-corner rectangle shape. An Activity will normally take some time to perform, will involve one or more resources from the organization, will usually require some type of *input*, and will usually produce some sort of *output*. Tasks and Sub-Processes are types of Activities.

Activity Life-Cycle:

A BPMN Activity goes through a series of *states* (its *life-cycle*) from the time that a *token* arrives until a *token* leaves the Activity. The types of states for an Activity include: *none, ready, active, cancelled, aborting, aborted, completing,* and *completed*. A single Activity instance will never go through all of these *states*.

Ad Hoc Process:

The Ad Hoc Process represents Processes where the Activities might occur in any order, and in any frequency—there is no specific ordering or obvious decisions.

Advanced BPMN Element:

These are BPMN elements that, we suggest, are used to model more complex behaviors. They are likely to be of most interest to those looking to automate Processes using a BPM Suite or Workflow environment.

Artifact:

Artifacts provide a mechanism to capture additional information about a Process, beyond the underlying flow-chart structure. There are three standard Artifacts in BPMN: Data Objects; Groups; and Text Annotations.

Assignment:

Assignments provide a mechanism to map data into an Activity as it is instantiated, and to update Process data based on the work of the Activity when it finishes. They also feature in Complex Gateways as a means to evaluate *conditions* and then control *token* flow. An *assignment* has two parts: a *condition* and an *action*. When an assignment is performed, it will evaluate the *condition* and if the *condition* is *true*, it then will perform the *action* such as updating the value of a Process or Data Object property. Do not confuse *assignment* attributes with the Performer attribute (used for role assignment).

Association:

Associations link (i.e. creates a relationship) one diagram object with another (such as Artifacts and Activities). Graphically it is represented as a dotted line (such as that connecting a Text Annotation to another object).

Atomic Activity:

An *atomic* Activity is a Task. They are the lowest level of detail presented in the diagram (i.e., they cannot be drilled-down upon to see a lower level of detail).

Black Box Pool:

A *black-box* Pool that is empty. That is, it does not contain a Process. The details of the Process are probably unknown to the modeler. Since it does not have any Process elements inside, any Message Flow going to or from the Pool must connect to its boundary.

Business Entity:

A *business entity* is one of the possible types of *participant*. Examples of *business entities* include IBM, FedEx, Wal-Mart, etc.

Business Process:

In BPMN a Business Process represents what an organization does—its work—in order to accomplish a specific purpose or objective.

Business Role:

A *business role* is one of the possible types of *participant*. Examples of *business roles* include buyer, seller, shipper, or supplier.

Catch:

Refers to the types of Events that wait for something to happen (e.g., the arrival of a *message*) before triggering. When they are triggered they allow the Process to continue. All Start Events and some Intermediate Events are *catch* Events.

Category:

A *category* is BPMN attribute common to all elements. It is used for analysis purposes. For example, Activities could be categorized as "customer valued" or "business valued." A Group is a graphical mechanism for to highlight a single *category*. Modeling tools may use other mechanisms (such as color).

Child Process:

A *child* Process is a Sub-Process that is contained within another Process. The relationship is from the perspective of the Process—it is the *parent* Process of the *child* Process.

Choreography:

A *choreography* process model is a definition of the expected behavior (a type of procedural contract or protocol) between interacting *participants*. In a flow chart format, it defines the sequence of interactions between two or more *participants*. A *choreography* will share many of the characteristics of an *orchestration* in that it will look like a process (i.e., a flow chart) and will include alternative and parallel paths, as well as Sub-Processes.

Collaboration:

Collaboration has a specific meaning in BPMN. Where a *choreography* defines the ordered set (a protocol) of *interactions* between *participants* (Pools), a *collaboration* just shows the *participants* and their *interactions*. A *collaboration* may also contain a one or more Processes (within the Pools).

Collapsed Sub-Process:

A *collapsed* Sub-Process is a Sub-Process where details of the Sub-Process are not visible in the diagram. Its appearance is the same as a Task with the addition of a small "+" sign at the bottom center of the shape.

Compensation:

Compensation relates to undoing work that been completed. It is modeled through Compensation Events and Activities. It is an automatic response to a cancellation of a *transaction*.

Complex Gateway:

Complex Gateways handle situations where the other types of Gateways do not provide support for the desired behavior. Modelers provide their own expressions that determine the merging and/or splitting behavior of the Gateway.

Compound Activity:

A *compound* Activity is a Sub-Process. They are non-*atomic* in the sense that you can open them up to see another level of process detail.

Condition:

A *condition* is a natural language or computer language expression that tests some data. The test will result in an answer of *true* or *false.*

Conditional Intermediate Event:

The Conditional Intermediate Event represents a situation where a Process is waiting for a pre-defined *condition* to become *true.*

Conditional Sequence Flow:

When a *condition* is used on the *outgoing* Sequence Flow of an Activity, it is called A Conditional Sequence Flow, and a mini-diamond (like a mini-Gateway) appears at the beginning of the Connector. When the Activity has completed <u>and</u> the *condition* evaluates to *true,* then a *token* (flow) will move down the Sequence Flow.

Conditional Start Event:

The Conditional Start Event represents a situation where a Process is started (i.e., triggered) when a pre-defined *condition* becomes *true.*

Connectors:

Connectors are lines that link two objects on a diagram. There are three different types of BPMN Connectors: Sequence Flow, Message Flow, and Associations.

Conversation:

A *conversation* interaction between two or more *participants* regarding a specific topic (such as a product or a customer request). There is no specific graphical support in BPMN for a *conversation* but the interaction may involve multiple Processes, *collaborations,* and/or *choreographies.* BPMN 2.0 is expected to have more support for this concept (including a specialized diagram).

Core BPMN Element:

These are the BPMN elements that we feel are most applicable to the needs of Business Analysts and business people. They can model the majority of Process behaviors.

Data Flow:

Data flow represents the movement of Data Objects from into and out of Activities. Graphically, directed Association connectors show the *data flow* between a Data Object and an Activity.

Data Object:

Data Objects represent the data and documents in a Process. Data Objects use a standard document shape (rectangle with one corner bent over). They usually define the *in-*

puts and *outputs* of Activities

Deadlock:

A *deadlock* is a situation where the flow of the Process cannot continue because a requirement of the model is not satisfied. For example, if a Parallel Gateway is expecting a *token* from all of its *incoming* Sequence Flow and one never arrives, the Process will deadlock.

Decision:

A point in the Process where one (or more) alternative paths is chosen. Decisions are implemented via Exclusive, Event, Inclusive, and Complex Gateways.

Default Sequence Flow:

A Sequence Flow that has a *default condition* and has a hatch mark near its beginning. The path for this Sequence Flow is chosen if the *conditions* for all the other *outgoing* Sequence Flow (from a Gateway or Activity) turn out to be *false*.

Delay:

In BPMN, delays are modeling with Timer Intermediate Events place in the *normal flow* of the Process. When the timer "goes off," then the Process can continue.

Downstream:

From the point of view of a BPMN element (e.g., a Task), the other elements which are connected through a Sequence Flow path in the direction where *tokens* <u>are going</u>, are considered *downstream*.

Embedded Sub-Process:

An *embedded* Sub-Process is actually part of the *parent* Process. They are not re-usable by other processes. All "process relevant data" used in the *parent* Process can also be referenced by the *embedded* Sub-Process (since it is part of the *parent*).

End Event:

An End Event marks where a Process, or more specifically, a "path" within a Process, ends. An End Event is a small, open circle with a single, thick lined boundary. There are eight different types of End Events: None, Message, Signal, Terminate, Error, Cancel, Compensation, and Multiple.

Error:

An *error* is generated when there is a critical problem in the processing of an Activity. *Errors* can be generated by applications or systems involved in the work (which are transparent to the Process) or by End Events.

Event:
> An Event is something that "happens" during the course of a Process. These Events affect the flow of the Process and usually have a *trigger* or a *result*. They can start, delay, interrupt, or end the flow of the Process (they either *throw* or *catch*). The three types of Events are: Start Events, Intermediate Events, and End Events.

Event Gateway:
> Event-Based Exclusive Gateways (or Event Gateway) represent an alternative branching point where the decision is based on <u>two or more Events</u> that might occur, rather than data-oriented *conditions* (as in an Exclusive Gateway).

Exception Flow:
> *Exception flow* is flow from the *outgoing* Sequence Flow from Intermediate Events that are attached to the boundaries of Activities, thereby interrupting the work of those Activities.

Exclusive Gateway:
> Exclusive Gateways are locations within a Process where there are two or more alternative paths. Based on the *conditions* on the Gateway's *outgoing* Sequence Flow, the Gateway will choose only one of the alternative paths (the first that evaluates to *true*).

Expanded Sub-Process:
> An *expanded* Sub-Process is a Sub-Process where the boundaries of the shape are extended to allow the display of the lower level details (i.e., a flow diagram appears within the Activity shape).

Flow Object:
> *Flow objects* are the elements that create the main structure of a Process. These elements are Activities, Events, and Gateways.

Gateway:
> Gateways are modeling elements that control Sequence Flow, as it diverges and converges within a Process—i.e. they represent points of control for the paths within the Process. All Gateways share the diamond shape.

Go-To Object:
> Go-To objects are paired Link Intermediate Events that enable Sequence Flow to "jump" from one place to another, often over large (screen or page) distances. The pair of Link

Events creates a *virtual* Sequence Flow.

Group:

A Group is a dashed, rounded rectangle used to surround a group of *flow objects* in order to highlight and/or categorize them.

Inclusive Gateway:

Inclusive Gateways support decisions where more than one outcome is possible at the decision point. The "O" marker identifies this type of Gateway.

Input:

An *input* is a Data Object or a Process *property* that is required for an Activity to begin work. Data Objects can be shown as *inputs* by a directed Association where they are the *source* of the connector.

Inputset:

An *inputset* is a collection of *inputs* that are all required for the Activity to begin work. An Activity may have more than one *inputset*. The first one that is complete (i.e., all the *inputs* are available) will trigger the start of the Activity (barring any other constraints).

Instance:

The start and performance of an Activity as an *instance* of an Activity or Process. For an Activity, a new *instance* is created whenever a *token* arrives at that Activity.

Interaction:

In BPMN, an *interaction* is a communication, in the form of a *message* exchange, between two *participants* of a *collaboration* or *choreography*. The *interaction* may involve one or more *messages*.

Intermediate Event:

An Intermediate Event is an Event that indicates where something happens/occurs after a Process has started and before it has ended. An Intermediate Event is a small, open circle with a double, thin lined boundary. There are nine types of Intermediate Events: None, Timer, Message, Signal, Error, Cancel, Compensation, Link, and Multiple.

Lane:

Lanes create sub-partitions for the objects within a Pool and often represent internal business roles within a Process. They provide a generic mechanism for partitioning the objects within a Pool based on characteristics of the elements.

Loops:

There are two types of *loops* in BPMN. Individual Activities can have looping characteristics (either While or Until). An assigned *condition* for the Activity determines if the performance of the Activity will be repeated. Alternatively, Sequence Flow can connect to an *upstream* object to create a loop in the Process flow.

Message:

A *message* is a direct communication between two business *participants*. *Messages* are different from *signals* in that they are directed between Process *participants*—i.e. they operate across Pools.

Message Flow:

Message Flow defines the messages/communications between two separate *participants* (shown as Pools) of the diagram. They are drawn with dashed lines that have a small hollow circle at the beginning and a hollow arrowhead at the end.

Multi-Instance Activities:

These are Activities, both Tasks and Sub-Processes, that are repeated based on a set of data (e.g., the number of orders on a list). The Activity does not loop, but has a set of separate instances, that may actually operate in parallel or serially (one after another).

Normal Flow:

The flow of a *token* between the *flow object*s, as they operate normally, is known as *normal flow*. Occasionally, however, an Activity will not operate normally. It might be interrupted by an Error or some other Event, and the resulting *token* flow is known as *exception flow*.

Off-Page Connector:

Off-page connectors are paired Link Intermediate Events that are used to place markers between printed pages of a model. The Events help the reader of the model find where a Sequence Flow ends on one page and starts up again on another page. This helps more when there are multiple Sequence Flow crossing the page boundaries.

Orchestration:

Within BPMN, *orchestration* models tend to imply a single coordinating perspective—i.e., they represent a specific business or organization's view of the process. As such, an *orchestration* Process describes how a single business entity goes about things.

Output:

An *output* is a Data Object or a Process *property* that is produced by an Activity when it is completed. Data Objects can be shown as *outputs* by a directed Association where they are the *target* of the connector.

Outputset:

An *outputset* is a collection of *outputs* that are all produced by the Activity when it is completed. An Activity may have more than one *outputset*. Only one of the *outputsets* is produced, but the decision as to which is handled by the work of the Activity and is transparent to the Process.

Parallel Gateway:

Parallel Gateways insert a split in the Process to create two or more parallel paths (threads). They can also merge parallel paths. The "+" marker is used to identify this type of Gateway.

Parent Process:

A *parent* Process is a Process that contains a Sub-Process. The relationship is from the Sub-Process's point of view. The Sub-Process is a *child* Process of the *parent* Process.

Participant:

Participants define a general business role, e.g. a buyer, seller, shipper, or supplier. Alternatively, they can represent a specific business entity, e.g. FedEx as the shipper. Each Pool can only represent <u>one</u> *participant*.

Pool:

A Pool acts as a container for a Process, each one representing a *participant* in a Business Process Diagram.

Process:

A Process in BPMN represents what an organization does—its work—in order to accomplish a specific purpose or objective. Most processes will require some type of input (either electronic or physical), use and/or consume resources, and produce some type of output (either electronic or physical).

Reusable Sub-Process:

A *reusable* Sub-Process is a separately modeled process that could be used in multiple contexts (e.g., checking the credit of a customer). The "process relevant data" of the *parent* (calling) Process is not automatically available to the Sub-Process. Any data must be transferred specifically, sometimes reformatted, between the *parent* and *child* Sub-Process.

Sequence Flow:

Sequence Flow connects and orders the Process *flow elements* (Activities, Events, and Gateways). Graphically, they are solid lines with solid arrowheads. Variations of Sequence Flow include Conditional Sequence Flow and Default Sequence Flow.

Signal:

A *signal* is analogous to a flare or siren; anyone who sees the flare or hears the siren may, or may not, react. They specialize BPMN Events (Start, Intermediate and End) to either broadcast or detect the *signal.*

Start Event:

A Start Event shows where a Process can begin. A Start Event is a small, open circle with a single, thin lined boundary. There are six types of Start Events: None, Timer, Message, Signal, Conditional, and Multiple.

Sub-Process:

A Sub-Process is a *compound* Activity used when the detail of the Process is broken down further (i.e. another Process). Thus, a "hierarchical" structure is possible with through the use of Sub-Processes. Being an Activity, it has a rounded-corner rectangle shape with a small "+" marker in the lower center of the shape.

Swimlanes:

Swimlanes help partition and/organize activities in a diagram. There are two main types: Pools and Lanes.

Task:

A Task is an *atomic* Activity that is used when the detail of the Process is not broken down further (i.e., into a lower-level Process). Being an Activity, it has a rounded-corner rectangle shape.

Text Annotation:

Text Annotations provide the modeler with the ability to add further descriptive information or notes about a Process or its elements.

Throw:

This refers to the types of Events that immediately produce a result (e.g., the sending of a *message*). All End Events and some Intermediate Events are *throw* Events.

Time-Out:

A *time-out* is a Timer Intermediate Event attached to the boundary of an Activity. If the timer "goes off" before the

Activity has completed, then the Activity is interrupted.

Timer:

A *timer* is a Timer Intermediate Event used as a *delay* or a *time-out*. The *timer* is set to a specific time and date or to a relative time and date.

Token:

A *token* is a "theoretical" object that we have used to create a descriptive "simulation" of the behavior of BPMN elements (it is not currently a formal part of the BPMN specification). *Tokens* theoretically move along Sequence Flow and pass through the other objects of the Process.

Top-Level Process:

Any Process that does not have a *parent* Process is considered a *top-level* Process—i.e., a Process that is not a Sub-Process is a *top-level* Process.

Transaction:

A Transaction is a formal business relationship and agreement between two or more *participants*. For a Transaction to succeed, all parties involved have to perform their own Activities and reach the point where all parties are agreed. If any one of them withdraws or fails to complete, then the Transaction cancels and all parties then need to *undo* all the work that has completed.

Trigger:

The circumstances that cause an Event to happen, such as the arrival of a *message* or a timer "going-off," are called *triggers*.

Upstream:

From the point of view of a BPMN element (e.g., a Task), the other elements which are connected through a Sequence Flow path in the direction where *tokens* are coming from, are considered *upstream*.

Index

Made in the USA
Lexington, KY
26 February 2015